The Secret
of
Self-Control

Crossway Books
by Dr. Richard L. Ganz

PsychoBabble:
The Failure of Modern Psychology—and the Biblical Alternative

The Secret of Self-Control:
What God Wants You to Know About Taking Charge of Your Life

The Secret
of
Self-Control

What God Wants You to Know
About Taking Charge of Your Life

Dr. Richard L. Ganz

CROSSWAY BOOKS • WHEATON, ILLINOIS
A DIVISION OF GOOD NEWS PUBLISHERS

The Secret of Self-Control

Copyright © 1998 by Dr. Richard L. Ganz

Published by Crossway Books
      a division of Good News Publishers
      1300 Crescent Street
      Wheaton, Illinois 60187

Cover design: D² DesignWorks

Writer-editor: Stephen W. Sorenson of Sorenson Communications,
      Colorado Springs, CO

First printing 1998

Printed in the United States of America

ISBN 1-58134-015-X

Library of Congress Cataloging-in-Publication Data
Ganz, Richard L., 1946-
    The Secret of self control : what God wants you to know about
  taking charge of your life / Richard Ganz.
       p.   cm.
  Includes bibliographical references and index.
  ISBN 1-58134-015-X
    1. Self-control—Religious aspects—Christianity. 2. Thought and
  Thinking—Religious aspects—Christianity. I. Title.
  BV4647.S39G36   1998
  248.8'6—dc21   98-20504

15	14	13	12	11	10	09	08	07	06	05	04	03	02	01	00
15	14	13	12	11	10	9	8	7	6	5	4	3	2

To my wife, Nancy—
my true friend in all things

Contents

Foreword

by John F. MacArthur, Jr.

Christianity in our generation has shown an ever-increasing obsession with self-esteem, self-image, self-acceptance—and a host of other self-isms. Self-love is something wrongly thought of as true spirituality these days.

At the same time, something no longer in fashion is the only legitimate fruit of the Spirit with a "self-" prefix: self-control.

Richard Ganz aims to remedy this imbalance in our thinking. This is a much-needed look at an important and often-neglected biblical truth.

Ganz's approach is biblical without being merely theoretical. Each chapter is intensely practical, offering instantly applicable help, not only for those seeking to regain control of an out-of-control life, but also for the average Christian who is weary of average living and eager to be an extraordinary man or woman of God.

The Christian notion of self-control is paradoxical. It's really a matter of being Spirit-controlled—so completely surrendered to the lordship of Christ and the will of God that our governing passions, our daily habits, and even our secret thoughts are godly rather than ungodly. Most Christians, if honest, would have to admit they fall far short of victory when it comes to that kind of self-control. And in a society where all self-control is neglected and often scorned, failure in this area is pervasive, even among longtime Christians.

Richard Ganz does a superb job of unwrapping and explaining the practical principles found in Scripture to help us gain and exercise the sort of self-control that Scripture says is the fruit of a life surrendered to the Holy Spirit (Galatians 5:16, 23).

Prepare yourself for a study that is at once challenging and uplifting. Ganz promises no fast and easy answers. There is no "quick fix" for learning self-control. In fact, people who insist on easy solutions to every problem doom themselves to failure in the area of self-control. But if you will patiently and consistently heed the advice in this book, a new, extraordinary life of Spirit-directed self-control will be yours.

PART ONE

⚘

How Do You Respond to Life's Challenges?

It's Your Choice!

1

The
Starting Point

*The starting point for taking control of your life is deter-
mining to live out your faith in Jesus Christ with passion,
integrity, and intensity. He desires to rule every inch of
your heart. When you live your life in submission to His
rule, He is able to change you into an extraordinary man
or woman.*

At the time I didn't realize the significant consequences of the simple
question I asked myself in 1979: *If I had a year to live, how would I
spend it?*

My wife and I had two beautiful children. We lived in a lovely
country cottage in the heart of a rural area of the United States. I was
teaching in a counseling program that cooperated with a leading seminary's theological training program. Life was going great!

The problem was, I realized that I wouldn't continue to do the
work I was doing if I had only a year to live. Then a deeper question
arose. *Why*, I wondered, *should I keep doing something I obviously
don't view as what I should do with my life—even if I have sixty years
in which to live?*

A new personal journey then began! My family and I ended up living above a barn in the mountains of Switzerland, where I had felt a
call to write a film script. We also experienced fifteen months of traveling and living out of the trunk of our car while I worked as an itin-
erant teacher/preacher. While it was an exciting time, it was a grueling
time for my wife. But through it we gained a sharpened focus of how

God was going to use us, even though once again it wasn't what either of us had ever imagined. In the process, we both had to wrestle through some tough issues, too.

You see, I began to understand how easy it is for me to deceive myself about my hopes, dreams, and aspirations. I began to understand how incredibly easy it would be to ignore the call of God and just live for self. If I hadn't realized this, I could have gone through my entire lifetime and never known that while my hopes, dreams, and aspirations are important, the call of God is of ultimate importance.

These experiences also compelled me to look at people in fresh ways, and what I saw startled me. I saw a lack of conviction and integrity in our society. Many people had given up living according to principles higher than self-indulgence and self-absorption. Furthermore, I came to believe that people have done this because they had given up on the only foundation from which absolute, transcendent principles for living can be derived—the Bible. Consequently, they have come to disregard principle, and men and women who possess character and principle simply don't fit into their world.

Do you remember when a man's word was his bond? He "struck hands," and no matter what happened, his word could be counted on— even if it cost him in some way. Today, in contrast, a person armed with a team of attorneys can sign a contract, and that means nothing because integrity is lacking. I'm sure you've met people who don't want to *be* honest; they just want to *appear* honest. They want to tout their honesty, but when the crunch comes, they are not prepared to be radically honest.

This crisis of integrity affects all of us in various ways. For example, burglars robbed the home of a friend of mine and stole many valuable possessions when he and his family were vacationing. As soon as he returned home, the police advised him to immediately call his insurance company. The insurance representative, in turn, told him to figure out the exact cost of the stolen items.

Later the insurance adjuster came by, went over the figures my friend and his wife presented, and said, "These seem fine. We'll be sending you 75 percent of this total."

"What do you mean?" my friend asked, surprised.

"It's a known fact that everyone inflates the prices of their stolen property," she replied, "and that the insurance company always gives 75 percent in order to adjust for that. And everyone accepts it."

"We will never accept 75 percent," my friend answered. "Before almighty God we arrived at these figures. We have put down our loss as carefully as we can, to the penny."

Confused, the adjuster explained that people were always slightly less than honest with adjusters.

My friend, in turn, explained that his family had to "stand before a far greater 'adjuster' than they would ever meet on this earth" and thus would never do what the adjuster had said was always done. A short time later the family received notice that they would be granted the entire amount of their claim even though the insurance company had never done that before.

This situation was a minor event in the lives of individuals who will never be known publicly and will probably never accomplish great things according to the world's standards. In fact, my friends would be surprised that I found their situation noteworthy. You see, they are committed to doing what is right "even when it hurts" in an age that generally lacks such commitment. Many people talk about honesty and integrity, but rarely does such talk go beyond a private or personal sentiment.

In fact, a well-known Christian who was hosting a Christian radio show introduced a commercial break by saying something like this: "You know, Thrifty Sam sells the best tires on the road. I wouldn't drive my car without them, and I hope you won't either." After the commercial break, he launched into his testimony by saying, "You know how sincere I am about Thrifty Sam's tires. Well, I'm just as sincere about the Gospel." He saw no problem in comparing his sincerity about the tires he was promoting to his sincerity for Jesus Christ.

This illustrates the real problem. Quite often Jesus isn't viewed as the eternal Lord and King who shatters evil and presumption. Instead, He is viewed as just another commodity, like car tires or batteries. And some of us find it all too easy to speak in the fashion of that Christian celebrity who owns great tires and has a great Savior. We don't care to realize that Jesus desires to rule every inch of our hearts. When we live our lives in submission to His rule, He is able to change us into extraordinary men and women.

Notice that I did not write that God necessarily wants us to *do* extraordinary things (although He may), but that He wants us to *be* extraordinary. According to *Webster's New World Dictionary*, the word *extraordinary* means "more or better than what is normal." God does not want us to be this way so we can boast about how great we are. He wants us to be this way because Jesus is extraordinary, and we are being made into His image.

It is an absolute contradiction to belong to Christ and yet live like the world and possess its values, drives, goals, and character. But, sad to say, this is just how many Christians live.

WHAT SETS EXTRAORDINARY PEOPLE APART?

Throughout the history of the Christian church, individuals such as the apostle Paul, the apostle Peter, Saint Augustine, Martin Luther, John Calvin, George Whitefield, John Wesley, Charles Spurgeon, and Francis and Edith Schaeffer have stood out prominently among God's people.

As we read through these names, we might be tempted to think that the apostle Paul was unique because he received God's direct revelation. But did he sit around waiting for revelation? I don't believe that he thought, *Life's a breeze. God speaks directly to me.* We need only to read the following passage to learn that he faced a number of difficult challenges: "I have worked," he wrote, "much harder, been in prison more frequently, been flogged more severely, and been exposed to death again and again. Five times I received from the Jews the forty lashes minus one. Three times I was beaten with rods, once I was stoned, three times I was shipwrecked, I spent a night and a day in the open sea" (2 Corinthians 11:23-25). And even if Paul had sat around, what about the rest of these people, of whom only Peter claimed to have received direct revelation from God?

What empowered these ordinary men to be extraordinary was their shared faith, which was deeply and pervasively rooted in Jesus their

Savior and Lord. They believed that God would truly move mountains when they exercised their faith. (See Matthew 17:20.) They shared what each of us, as a Christian, is supposed to have—a *living* faith. This living faith dominated everything else in their lives, which they lived out with passion and intensity. Living by faith became their goal, their reason for being. Nothing else mattered much to them.

Also, as new believers, they found themselves facing dramatically new situations. What separated them from the rest of the people in their generations was this: They carefully determined how to accomplish what they believed God had called them to do in their new situations. They no longer viewed themselves as *career-oriented people;* they were *called people*. They directed everything they did to the accomplishment of that calling. Seeking to implement their vision, they worked, prayed, and planned according to the Word of God.

When we think about them in this way, what is perhaps most amazing is that the world was changed because of them. They lived out a simple faith in Christ, but how it changed them—and the world! Without God they were fear-ridden, prone to deny their Lord to save their own necks. With Him they turned the world of their day upside down—after they had been changed from the inside out. They weren't elitist believers. They simply acted on the faith that had shaken their whole being.

Consider another dramatic example of living faith—demonstrated by Elijah when he confronted the 450 false prophets of Baal. As the story unfolded, Elijah met King Ahab and asked him to summon people from throughout Israel to meet him on Mount Carmel and to bring the 450 prophets of Baal who ate at wicked Queen Jezebel's table. When the meeting convened, Elijah challenged the Israelites to either follow God or Baal. "But the people said nothing" (1 Kings 18:21).

So Elijah set up a test. The 450 prophets of Baal were to choose a bull to sacrifice, and he would do the same. Each bull would be cut into pieces and placed on a separate wooden altar. "Then you call on the name of your god," Elijah stated, "and I will call on the name of the Lord. The god who answers by fire—he is God" (1 Kings 18:24).

The Israelites and the prophets agreed to this test, and all morning the prophets of Baal called on their god and danced around their altar. But Baal didn't answer. So Elijah taunted them. "Shout louder!" he called out. "Perhaps he is deep in thought, or busy, or traveling. Maybe he is sleeping and must be awakened" (1 Kings 18:27).

The prophets of Baal shouted louder and continued to prophesy frantically. Still nothing happened.

In the evening Elijah called the Israelites to his side and repaired the ruined altar of the Lord, using twelve stones that represented the twelve tribes of Israel. He then arranged the wood, cut up the bull, and laid it on the altar. Then three times the people poured four large jars of water onto the bull and the altar until water ran everywhere.

Elijah then called upon God to answer him so the people would know that He was God in Israel. Immediately God's fire burned up the sacrifice, the wood, the twelve stones, the water, and even the nearby soil. Shortly thereafter Elijah had the 450 false prophets executed.

Do you know what I find particularly exciting about this example of faith? As we read in James 5:17, "Elijah was a man just like us."

A TRAGEDY

When we consider how God used Elijah and other men and women of God throughout the ages, it's tragic that Christians today sit around and seem to let life pass them by. Do you ever feel as if that's happening to you?

You can get rid of the hindrances in your life and experience life the way God intends it to be. A life of unimaginable joy and fulfillment awaits you as a child of God as you allow the passionate, life-changing faith you possess to run its course through you.

It's not just fulfilling our dreams that's vital. It's being people who have vision. Solomon clearly emphasized that there can be no lasting contribution without a vision: "Where there is no vision, the people perish" (Proverbs 29:18, KJV).

At a time when the pressures of secularism, materialism, and selfism loom so large in our society, the character of Christ is being squeezed out of the people of God.

In this book I'll challenge you to take charge of your life, to become dominated by a living faith in God. My desire is to help you as a Christian to know who you are and, more importantly, to know who you are meant to be.

Nothing can keep you and me from living lives of power, meaning, and vibrancy, from making decisions based on the transcendent, biblical principles that should guide our lives. These principles determine where each of us can serve and the ways in which we can serve. When we decide to live by them, we are freed up to live with passion and principle, joy and calling.

Now let's look at how we can make a new beginning, take charge of our lives and discover what the overcoming life is all about.

PAUSE FOR REFLECTION

1. If you had one year to live, would you live differently? Why or why not?

_____

_____

_____

_____

2. Have your hopes, dreams, and aspirations been an important part of your life? If so, why? If not, why not?

_____

_____

_____

_____

3. Write down a few words that define your faith in God right now. Be honest.

_____

_____

_____

4. Now that you see that description on paper, how would you like your faith in God to be different?

_____

_____

_____

_____

Begin Taking Charge Today

Today you have the opportunity to begin taking charge of your life. You can stop making rationalizations and justifications that keep you from being all you can be and from facing your problems. But the process will require you to face your beliefs, thoughts, and actions honestly.

Many people assume that they are powerless to change anything about themselves. They feel as if they have little or no control over their lives and that their best efforts at improving and reforming themselves are thwarted by who and what they are and/or by their circumstances—ones they have created or ones created by others. These "powerless" people are almost never able to become what they want to be and quite often become what they deep down despise.

They try to feel their way through a culture filled with too many "to-do's," and the pressure builds when they can't get everything done. They set high expectations for themselves, only to experience what they consider to be failure. Bombarded by mass amounts of information, they also face a plethora of new devices and technologies that have changed everything we deal with in life—from how weeds are trimmed to the very definitions of life and death.

Lacking the standards of ethical decision-making and truth that can only come from the Bible and a personal relationship with God through Jesus Christ, many of these people fruitlessly attempt to determine which truths to live by and which standards to implement for decision-making. But the relativistic foundation on which they build their lives shifts like sand.

Can you relate? Have you felt powerless? Have you had difficulty recognizing who you are called to be or even who you want to become? If so, you are certainly not alone.

Millions of people respond to their problems and apparent powerlessness by getting depressed. According to some estimates, about 25 percent of the population of Canada and the United States is at least mildly depressed at any given moment.[1]

That's about 75 million people! Contrary to what we might think, people who were born before World War II experience far less depression than the Baby Boomers. Why is this? I believe the answer is really quite simple. As this century progressed, life became more and more complicated even though such timesavers as washing machines, dryers, and toaster ovens were introduced. People began running here and there at a faster pace.

Other factors also helped to create a climate of busyness and confusion. Modern medicine and science developed new devices and technologies. Carried along by the momentum the war had created, industry thrived. The standard of living rose. At the same time the foundation of biblical truth was seriously challenged. Thus people born after the war obtained many material things but lacked a strong foundation rooted in biblical truth.

As people struggled for equilibrium, a state of depression emerged over society as a whole. Dr. Gerald Klerman, the former director of the U.S. Alcohol, Drug Abuse, and Mental Health Agency, coined this age the Age of Melancholy.

In addition to the many in our culture suffering from depression, many others experience deep anxiety and fear or try to use materialism, sex, food, or work to ease their pain and fill the void in their lives. Newspapers are filled with articles about people—even children—who turn to violence in order to have a sense of power.

Should it be surprising, then, that so many people—including Christians—commit suicide, become dependent on antidepressant drugs, or remain in long-term therapy? It's easy to get into despair these days and hard to get out.

IT'S TIME TO TAKE CONTROL OF YOUR LIFE

Perhaps you feel impotent to fight against the rage or despair you feel so often. You may feel that you don't really know who you are, but you don't have to give up. You don't have to turn to criminal behavior to gain power. You don't have to memorize clichés that are somehow supposed to turn your life around. You may not have to spend years going to a psychological professional who helps you interpret and resolve repressed childhood conflicts buried deeply within your subconscious mind. You may not even have to face the side effects of taking antidepressant medicine or undergoing electroconvulsive therapy.[2]

There is another way! It lies in taking charge of the only person you can control—yourself! Today, with God's help, you can start taking charge of your life. You can stop making rationalizations that keep you from being all you were meant to be.

But, you may be thinking, *I don't know who I am supposed to be. I don't know how to take control. I don't know how to stop being a victim and face my problems.* If that's in your mind right now, that's okay. Each of us has to start somewhere. So let's start at the easiest place.

THE PLACE OF RECOGNITION

Consider the following four points carefully.

1. You have to want to change your life. I'm willing to help you, as other people probably are. But the motivation has to come from within you.

2. Recognize that you are exceptional. God has created no one exactly like you. Your life can have a godly impact on other people, even if you don't see that impact during your lifetime.

3. God will empower you as you seek to take control of your life. The Holy Spirit is the one who works the changes in you and makes you "a new creation" (2 Corinthians 5:17). Although you can try to make

changes within yourself on your own, remember that a God-changed character is very different from a self-driven, self-changed character.

4. Reaching your potential requires commitment. Exceptional people who may do exceptional things usually put a great deal of effort and practice into achieving specific goals. Godly men and women, for example, dedicate themselves to knowing God and His Word.

Many Christians want to become "super-spiritual." They want to know the Bible well, enjoy a deep walk with God, and see God working in their lives daily. Sad to say, a number of them want an easy fix. They are not willing to put in the effort necessary to accomplish these goals. But like superior athletes who spend years training for just one Olympic race, exceptional Christians have to submit to spiritual training. There are no shortcuts.

We all remember the 1994 Olympics. Tanya Harding was placed in competition with Nancy Kerrigan, who was a better figure skater. Apparently Ms. Harding arranged for someone to try to ruin Nancy's career. And many of us read about the mother who tried to get a cheerleader killed so that her own daughter could be in the limelight. Fortunately these incidents are not typical, but they do reflect the tendency people have to try to receive benefits without deserving them.

CHANGING YOUR RESPONSES TO DIFFICULTIES

If you are prepared to do some work on yourself, the results will be well worth your effort. But you may need direction as to how to proceed. That's where I would like to help you. I can show you how to break through seemingly insurmountable impasses in your life. The process will require you to face your beliefs, thoughts, and actions honestly.

An impasse is often nothing more than our ineffective behavior multiplied by countless trials and errors that leave us feeling helpless. Based on our past failures, we come to believe that we've done all we can do, which elicits another "failure response." So we quit trying to take charge of our lives, quit believing that we can face our difficulties and regain control of our lives.

But this is wrong thinking and action! Just as you and I are capable of confessing and repenting of foolish, sinful behavior, we are capable of replacing a failure response with one that will lead us to victory and hope, joy and positive change. As we develop better responses, we will obtain the flexibility to learn how to control our responses (that often get us into trouble). Even more important, we'll learn to choose how we will respond to difficulties that have often devastated us in the past.

Let me explain this by using a simple illustration. Let's say that an executive is often asked to give oral presentations during important meetings. Every time the executive gets up to speak, he or she gets wet, clammy skin and shaky, wobbly knees. This nervousness makes the presentation less effective. And the same scenario occurs over and over again.

The executive is accomplished in achieving emotional and physical responses that communicate the expectation of failure, right? Then when the executive does not do well, he or she is not disappointed. But what if the executive learns to respond more appropriately? Think about how much better he or she will feel about getting up in front of the team—and how much better the presentation will probably be!

My oldest daughter, a college student, recently struggled with whether or not to switch majors. She was a straight-A student and clearly on the way to receiving full scholarships to various graduate schools. But she had never taken a course in the new area she was considering and had no guarantee of success in that direction.

When she and I talked about this decision, she stated, "I don't feel that I'll ever use what I'm studying now to really help people. But I know that I'll always sail through, and I recognize that I may not do well in these other courses." As we talked more, she realized that fear of failure was keeping her from trying something she felt called to pursue. She changed her response, switched majors, and didn't allow herself to live in fear. She may not do as well in the new area of study, but she is willing to try. She has chosen to live by faith.

When I mention that each of us can learn to choose our responses to difficulties and not be gripped by former destructive patterns, people in my seminars sometimes admit that they are afraid of losing their spontaneity and becoming like robots. As we talk further, they realize that's nonsense.

Do you want to stay trapped in crippling fear, anxiety, or panic? Do you want to wander aimlessly through life in terror of situations you'll face? It is far better to learn how to master the myriad of troubles that come your way.

If being your own person before God is important to you, take charge of your life! Choose to gain control over who you are instead of being controlled by everything that you say you hate—or at least strongly dislike. (I would even suggest that you don't really hate or even dislike those controlling factors. In fact, think about the many perceived benefits they bring you that seemingly make it worthwhile for you to hang onto them, even when you think or say that the opposite is true.)

If deep inside you truly want to be free of the snares and stressors that choke your life, you can be free! We all tend to be creatures of habit. At some time all of us have seen that our best intentions fall flat—again and again—and we respond accordingly. When we learn bad habits, they can seem impossible to break. But when we learn good habits, they can also be hard to break.

Soon I'll show you how to put off habitual, destructive patterns of response and replace them with righteous, beautiful, and excellent ones. But right now, let's look at several basic patterns of response that all people use to one degree or another. The following self-destructive responses have one thing in common—they keep us from experiencing the kind of life God intends for us to have.

The Minimizing Pattern

I'll use a college student as an example, but these same truths apply to people in all walks of life. When he or she comes into the dormitory after receiving a bad grade on a final examination, the minimizing student says simply, "Oh well, I shouldn't worry. Grades don't matter anyway."

The Permanentizing Pattern

This student says, "My situation in that class is horrible, my life is horrible, everything is horrible, and it's always going to be horrible. And I'll never get a good grade again."

The Destroying Pattern

Refusing to face the situation honestly, this student destroys anyone connected with it. "I'm just a stupid, incompetent kid," he or she says. Or, "My professor is a complete jerk."

The Retaliating Pattern

This student doesn't minimize, permanentize, or destroy. All he or she cares about is getting even, with a vengeance, for what he or she perceives the professor did. When he or she fails a course, it's viewed as a personal insult.

A P.A.T. ANSWER THAT WORKS

Perhaps some of you hope that I'm going to offer magical solutions that can automatically make everything okay in your life and teach you certain ways to respond that will guarantee you an overcoming life.

I'm not. There are no effective magical answers that do not involve all that you believe, think, and do. But there is another easy way of responding that is contrary to the patterns of response I've just mentioned. I call this "P.A.T. answer" a *maximizer*. It contains three parts.

"P"—Problem: Understanding the Problem

During a snowstorm I moved our car down our quarter-mile country lane to make sure I'd be able to get out about an hour later and travel to a conference. I didn't want to come out in knee-deep snow and discover that the car was stuck. But when I gingerly pushed on the gas pedal to return to the house, the car didn't move. I had a *problem!*

"A"—Attitude: Choosing the Appropriate Attitude Toward the Problem

I sat in the car wondering, *How could this happen to me when I'm so busy? I've handled this entire situation correctly. I planned ahead to make sure I wouldn't get stuck. This can't happen.* So I tried again and heard that sickening sound of tires spinning on what had become ice.

As I exhausted myself running through a snowy field to get home, my next response was anger—at myself, at my car, at the snow, which was greatly inconveniencing me. I even became angry at the lane for causing me so much difficulty.

When I stormed through the door and saw my wife happily working, I became impatient, frantic, and self-centered in the way I communicated the situation.

"T"—Technique: Choosing the Best Resolution

Nancy kindly agreed to stop what she was doing and help me, and we went outside. Despite our best efforts, the tires continued to spin.

"Where are those orange things you bought years ago with the claws that dig into the ice so the tires can move?" Nancy asked.

I hadn't been able to find them for years, but she had given me a new idea. *What can I use?* I thought. So I tried another technique. I pulled out carpeting from the trunk and placed it under the tires. Soon the tires flung the carpet onto the snow, and the car still didn't move.

My next attempt to find the right technique was to jam a tree limb under the tires. But that didn't work either.

As I stood there angry, frustrated, depressed, and sweaty, a car stopped, and someone asked if he could lend us a hand. Within seconds the car was free. But until that moment, I felt as if my day was ruined. Worse yet, I could have ruined Nancy's day. And if my kids had been home, I might have ruined their day, too.

But—and here's the point—it was not necessary to allow a stuck car to ruin my day. Are you with me? One horrible experience didn't have to make the entire day horrible.

My attitude toward getting stuck caused me to think, *How can this be happening? I'll never get out of this. Everything has to stop and revolve around my problem.* But what if I had shut off the engine as soon as my tires began to spin, prayed for wisdom from God, and said aloud, "This is no big deal. I'll just flag down the next person who comes by, and I'll get out in no time"?

EVALUATE YOUR PATTERNS OF RESPONSE

We all face problems. Life is filled with them. Some of us think through our problems and create a plan for solving them. Others of us react to them without much thought. And when we respond in reactive ways again and again, we set up a reactive rather than a thoughtful pattern of response.

Reactors create far more stress than thinkers because reactors' solutions to their problems are far less effective. This means more trouble will be created, which will lead to more problems, which will cause reacting people to fly around and react to one thing after another and accomplish virtually nothing.

When God revealed in Scripture that we can be of good cheer even when we face serious problems, He obviously knew that problems are building blocks for our character development. "Suffering," we read in Romans 5:3-4, "produces perseverance; perseverance, character; and character, hope."

In my case, when I spoke with Nancy about the pattern of response I'd exhibited when faced with the car stuck in the snow, she said, "You respond that way so often."

I didn't want to hear that. But she was right. I had become trapped in a wrong pattern of response. I began to see that with God's help I could break that pattern. I realized the importance of evaluating a problem situation, recognizing my attitudes toward it, and devising a better technique to deal with it.

Just as I had a choice whether or not to learn and apply new attitudes to my difficulties, I had the choice to develop character or damage my character. You have the same choice. Will you determine right now to use the problems in your life to grow? Will you commit yourself to take charge even when your life seems to be charging out of control?

PAUSE FOR REFLECTION

1. List three problems you have faced recently and the attitudes with which you faced each of them. Then list the techniques you used to try to handle each problem. List honestly what happened and how you really responded.

_____

_____

_____

_____

Do you see any patterns of response emerging? If so, what are they?

_____

_____

_____

_____

2. Consider each of the following situations. For each one, list the Problem and then write down the Attitude(s) you'd typically have toward each situation and the Technique(s) you'd typically try to apply in order to solve the problem.

• The principal calls to say that your child just got into another fight at school.

_____

_____

_____

_____

• A person with a cart full of groceries cuts in front of you in the supermarket line.

_____

_____

_____

_____

• You are overlooked for a significant promotion at work. Everyone agrees that the person who received the new position has much less ability than you.

_____

_____

_____

_____

• You and your wife have a battle over finances.

_____

_____

_____

_____

3

Applying the A.N.S.W.E.R. Tool to Your Life

As you learn to use this tool, you will build a deeper relationship with God and gain greater control over your life.

Each of us faces problems, and sometimes our circumstances seem to be hurtling out of control. In the last chapter, we looked at the Problem, the Attitude, and the Technique—P.A.T. Now we're going to look at the A.N.S.W.E.R. This tool sets the stage for the rest of this book. The principles identified by each of these six letters will help you gain greater control over your life.

A—APPEAL TO THE LORD

Suppose I ask you, "Do you believe that trusting God is an important part of your relationship with God?" If you are a Christian, you'd agree, right? But why do so many Christians who are facing problems consult God last? In reality they should go to God first, even before they consult a doctor, an attorney, a teacher, an accountant, and so on.

God is to be our starting point when we face difficulties. "Cast all your anxiety on him because he cares for you," the apostle Peter wrote (1 Peter 5:7). David wrote, "As for God, his way is perfect; the word of the Lord is flawless. He is a shield for all who take refuge in him"

(Psalm 18:30). Jeremiah quoted the Lord, who said, "Call to me and I will answer you and tell you great and unsearchable things you do not know" (Jeremiah 33:3). The apostle Paul wrote, "Do not be anxious about anything, but in everything, by prayer and petition, with thanksgiving, present your requests to God" (Philippians 4:6).

It makes great sense to begin with the God who loves you! He will always walk alongside you, will help you, and will be your advocate. Are you appealing to Him when you face difficulties?

N—DETERMINE YOUR NONNEGOTIABLE BELIEFS

As we'll see, everyone deals with problems in a context, which includes a system of beliefs. So it's important that you think about the aspects of your personal belief system that you will never compromise or alter—not even a little bit. When you know what you believe, you can stick by it. You can prepare yourself to be faithful to your beliefs—in your thoughts, spoken words, and actions.

Consider these true illustrations:

• Harold knew it was time to change jobs. He was offered a great job that required him to work at least two Sundays a month. Some people might think that this would be a small price to pay for a superior job, but he refused to consider the offer because he held the conviction that it was wrong for him to work on Sundays.

• Robert, a young salesman, received pressure from his manager to sell customers audiovisual materials they didn't need and to do virtually anything to close a sale. Valuing integrity, he continued to keep his customers' best interests in mind and eventually chose a different career.

• Karen spoke to me about her relationship with Michael. "He is exactly what I've always dreamed of," she said. "He is considerate, sensitive, and a good listener. He is handsome and about to be promoted to a higher management level. But he's not a Christian." Many people never think about this issue, but for Karen this point became central. Even though she should have considered it earlier in their relationship, she realized that she would not marry a non-Christian.

• A teenager caught off guard by a school principal who demanded to know the truth about a situation, answered, "I don't know." But he did know, and later on he became upset because he had overstepped a nonnegotiable belief—always to tell the truth.

Many years ago the Davy Crockett television show was popular. Davy tried to conduct his actions based on this slogan: "Be sure you are right; then go ahead." When you define what God says is right (and for Christians that involves studying the Bible, praying, talking with other Christians, and so on), you can act on it.

Our beliefs are the substance out of which everything else flows. Our beliefs motivate and dominate all that we are and all that we do. If you believe you are a failure, for instance, everything you do will substantiate that belief and cause it to come true. Or you will die trying to prove to everyone that you are not a failure. Likewise, if you believe that God is with you and seek His will for your life, you will have hope.

What we believe is powerful. Regardless of what you think about hypnosis, it's interesting to note that hypnotized individuals are able to do many unusual things through posthypnotic suggestion. In a 1958 *Science Digest* article, Dr. Theodore Barber wrote, "The [hypnotized] subject behaves differently because he thinks and believes differently. . . . When a subject believes that he is deaf, he behaves as if he is deaf. . . . When he is convinced that he is insensitive to pain, . . . he can undergo surgery without anesthesia."

Although we'll explore the power of belief later in more detail, I'll share one more illustration. When I worked in a psychiatric hospital, nearly all of the patients had one thing in common—they believed they were crazy, and this belief caused them to live accordingly. One of the most powerful things I'd do for them was to communicate that I truly believed they were not crazy. When they came to believe that, it often changed their lives.

When I asked one patient, Tom, what his problem was, he answered, "I'm mentally ill." When I asked how he had arrived at this assessment, he described how he had removed all his clothes, burned his college books in the campus square, and danced around the fire until the police took him to the psychiatric hospital. But as we talked further, he saw that he had responded sinfully to the pressures of university life. Sin, not illness, had overtaken him. His change of belief led to his eventual release from the psychiatric ward.

S—DEVELOP YOUR STRATEGY

What is a strategy? It's a method used to obtain an advantage—during wartime, in business or politics, and in many other situations. Many companies, for instance, create business strategies—ways to create new markets, increase profitability, improve customer service, and so on.

I am not talking about the word *strategy* in the context of gaining advantage over another person. I'm talking about obtaining an advantage for yourself so that you can, with God's help, take charge of your life and be prepared for the spiritual warfare all Christians face.

Paul taught an important lesson on strategy when he wrote in 2 Corinthians 10:3-4, "For though we live in the world, we do not wage war as the world does. The weapons we fight with are not the weapons of the world. On the contrary, they have divine power to demolish strongholds." Paul recognized that human weapons are useless in spiritual warfare. Christians need to utilize spiritual weapons to combat Satan, to pursue God's strategies, and to allow those strategies to unfold according to His plan.

God's strategy is never accountable to human reason. Did it make sense for the Israelites to walk around Jericho, a walled city, for seven days and then blow trumpets to make the walls fall down (Joshua 6)? Did it make sense to ask Gideon to take 300 selected men and rout more than 100,000 Midianites (Judges 6—7)? Did it make sense for a lowly shepherd boy to use a slingshot against Goliath, a giant warrior who was nine feet, nine inches tall and whose armor weighed about 125 pounds (1 Samuel 17)?

Goliath was insulted by David's strategy and said, "Am I a dog, that you come at me with sticks?" David replied that he had come "in the name of the Lord Almighty."

When we have appealed to God and identified our nonnegotiable beliefs, our strategies for living become vital. We can take action and be confident that God is with us when we face "giants" in our lives.

Most people, unfortunately, go through life without having a plan. They just try to get through each day. But is that all there is to life? The slogan says: "Life is hard, and then you die." Is there nothing more?

In my book *You Shall Be Free Indeed*, I share an illustration I'd like to repeat. A logger in the wilderness of northern Canada became lost one bitterly cold evening. Seeing lights in the distance, he rushed toward them, only to stop in terror when he had to cross a river. It seemed frozen, but as he walked on it, he began to think he could hear the ice cracking. So he walked more carefully and slowly.

Eventually he began crawling inch by inch toward the other side. Sweat poured down his face. Then he heard the distant sound of bells. The sound grew louder, and soon a horse-drawn wagon filled with singing loggers crossed the ice. As if in a dream, the logger stood up, shook himself off, and ran the rest of the way to the other side of the river.

Both the wagon's occupants and the terrified logger made it from point A to point B. The only difference is in *how they got there!*

The same truth applies to your life. Will you get from point A to point B consumed by fear, panic, and/or despair? Or will you go with singing and with sleigh bells ringing?

W—DISCOVERING THE WAY OF WISDOM

Solomon wrote, "There is a way that seems right to a man, but in the end it leads to death" (Proverbs 16:25). What a contrast between this result and the one Moses described: "Now choose life, so that you and your children may live" (Deuteronomy 30:19). The Bible contrasts the way that only *seems* right with the way that *is* right. Moses went on to detail that the right way is to "love the Lord your God, listen to his voice, and hold fast to him" (Deuteronomy 30:20).

Consider another contrast: "The fear of the Lord is the beginning of wisdom" (Psalm 111:10) and "fools despise wisdom and discipline" (Proverbs 1:7).

In Proverbs God revealed that a person living in the way of wisdom will be saved from the ways of wicked people (2:12) and from immorality (2:16), will be directed down the path of righteousness (2:20), will receive added years to his or her life and be prosperous (3:2), will experience physical health (3:8) and peace (3:17), will be delivered from fear and will sleep soundly (3:24), and will gain confidence in God and avoid being ensnared (3:26). And this list could go on and on!

The "way-of-wisdom" theme winds its way throughout Scripture. No biblical writer expressed the benefits of wisdom more succinctly than Solomon, who wrote, "Wisdom is supreme; therefore get wisdom" (Proverbs 4:7).

If your life seems to be out of control, the answer doesn't lie in some mysterious, ethereal, mystical revelation of a deep, unconscious, archetypal experience. The answer lies in the way of truth—the wisdom of God.

E—RECEIVING EMPOWERMENT FROM GOD

Now that you have appealed to God, discovered your nonnegotiable beliefs, planned your strategy, and committed yourself to implementing it with wisdom, you are ready to see how such a process can lead to complete empowerment in your life.

Scripture calls you and me to be full of God's power. The Bible teaches that "we have this treasure in jars of clay to show that this all-surpassing power is from God and not from us" (2 Corinthians 4:7). Paul communicated this truth again in 2 Corinthians 12:9, when he recorded what God had said to him: "'My grace is sufficient for you, for my power is made perfect in weakness.'"

God delights in our availability and will empower us. He doesn't need us but chooses to use us for His service. Service is the channel for the power of God, the means by which our naturally selfish lives can be refocused.

We are never to become self-reliant or try to become a power unto ourselves. Rather, when the pressures get "far beyond our ability to endure," as Paul put it (2 Corinthians 1:8), we realize that God allows those pressures to occur so that we will learn to trust in Him, not in ourselves. We can then learn that the power of God is the only real power to pursue.

When Jesus and the disciples faced tremendous pressure before His ascent to heaven, He said, "You will receive power when the Holy Spirit comes on you; and you will be my witnesses in Jerusalem, and in all Judea and Samaria, and to the ends of the earth" (Acts 1:8).

Soon afterward the apostles stood in stark contrast to everyone else around them. After Peter and John healed the crippled beggar (Acts 3), for example, the authorities were forced to ask them, "By what power or what name did you do this?" (Acts 4:7).

In response Peter and John answered that it was "by the name of Jesus Christ of Nazareth, whom you crucified but whom God raised from the dead, that this man stands before you healed" (Acts 4:10).

The empowerment you will receive from God is not something you can sustain yourself. It doesn't come from you or your efforts; it comes from the work of Jesus Christ and the Holy Spirit. Luke next explained what this power is to be used for: "With great power the apostles continued to testify to the resurrection of the Lord Jesus" (Acts 4:33). God gives this power to Christians for the purpose of bringing people to a saving relationship with Christ.

Sometimes this empowerment leads to other consequences. Remember Stephen, the church's first martyr, who was "full of God's grace and power" (Acts 6:8)? He was infused with God's power, but the religious leaders of his day ended up stoning him to death (Acts 7).

It's easy to believe that only people who have professional degrees or technical excellence can help hurting persons. Certainly counselors, for instance, help people, but such counselors can never be substitutes for the power of God, which can enable any of us to reach out with hope to other people. Paul, in fact, prayed, "May the God of hope fill you with all joy and peace as you trust in him, so that you may overflow with hope by the power of the Holy Spirit" (Romans 15:13).

This power from God is not something for which you have to wait. If you are a Christian, you already possess His power. You have passed from spiritual darkness into the light of God. Christians who live in spiritual weakness do so because their eyes are not focused properly. Instead of looking at what is true, they fixate on their difficult problems, which can only lead to disaster. Let me illustrate what I mean.

Recently my daughter won a free winter-hazard driving lesson from a company that offers a driver-training program. Since she could not attend, I took her place. The teacher showed a video involving a skid and pointed out that the main reason the car remained in the skid was that the driver kept his eyes focused on where the skidding car was going. In order to get out of the skid, he should have fixed his eyes in the direction he desired the car to go—not in the direction of the skid. The right maneuver requires tremendous effort and concentration, but it can save the life of someone who learns it.

Many people go through life in the skids. They focus on their skids. They put great effort into their skids. They hope fervently that their skids will be reduced, yet live as if they have no control over the direction of their lives. With that approach, it's no surprise that their lives consist of one skid after another. Even the name of the place where society's down-and-outers wind up is called Skid Row.

How can we as Christians get out of our skids? We can focus in the direction in which we want to go. The writer of Hebrews recorded this instruction: "Let us fix our eyes on Jesus" (Hebrews 12:2). These words were written just after the heroes of the faith were mentioned in Hebrews 11. These heroes were flogged, chained, stoned, imprisoned, and put to death. Clearly we are to understand that the power of God doesn't keep us from difficult experiences. It does, however, enable us to go through them triumphantly and with hope.

After encouraging us to focus on Christ, the writer of Hebrews challenged believers to resist sin, take discipline seriously, remain encouraged, endure hardship, strengthen themselves, live in peace, be holy, and worship God "with reverence and awe" (Hebrews 12:28).

Quite a few Christians believe that only "superpeople" can achieve these goals, that ordinary believers will be left far back in the pack because the struggle to change will be too hard. But the Scriptures teach that we can accomplish incredible things because "God did not give us a spirit of timidity, but a spirit of power, of love and of self-discipline" (2 Timothy 1:7).

God calls you and me to be men and women of courage, character, power, love, and self-discipline. That, without a doubt, is what God's empowerment is all about. Many of us want empowerment for the wrong reasons. We want it for what we think it will enable us to *do* rather than for what it will enable us to *be*.

When God empowers us, He completes our character. Remember, "suffering produces perseverance; perseverance, character" (Romans 5:3-4). God is concerned with our character as well as our behavior.

R—CHOOSING OUR RESPONSE

In my counseling practice, troubled counselees consistently fail in observable ways because they think that they have only two options—do everything right or do nothing at all to promote personal change. They fail to grasp that doing nothing will only cause continued failure and that doing everything may be unrealistic and even humanly unattainable.

For example, a depressed woman I'll call Helen came with her husband to be counseled. When I asked her to describe her depression, she answered, "My home is a complete wreck. I have six children, the youngest of whom is a toddler. If I don't get things under control, I'll remain depressed forever." As it turns out, she had tried to organize the entire house, and after an hour's effort had sat down—defeated, exhausted, and more depressed.

Certainly various things were happening in her life on a biological, hormonal, emotional, and spiritual level. But it was easy for me to see how her all-or-nothing mentality had thrown her deeper into despair as she faced the inevitable defeat of trying to complete her housework within sixty minutes.

So I discovered what Helen believed to be her easiest, more difficult, and most difficult household responsibilities. We then worked together to create a program that helped her and her husband cope with the mountain of responsibilities. She started with the easiest one—all she did one day was dust. Then the next day she washed that day's laundry. During day three she vacuumed the upstairs. She also saw her husband begin to help.

You know what happened? Within weeks she was transformed. She had accomplished real success. She had realized that she could accomplish meaningful tasks, and that encouraged her to try harder. "I have accomplished more in just one week," she exclaimed happily, "than I have during the past two years!"

I can summarize why that simple system worked so well for Helen by telling a story about professional basketball coach Pat Riley—the coach whose teams have won the most professional basketball games in history. When he was coaching the Los Angeles Lakers in 1985, they had a great year but didn't win the NBA championship. The next season did not seem to offer great prospects, so team members began thinking, *We've given it everything, and there's nothing more we can give. If we didn't win last season, how can we win now?*

Pat devised a plan. He challenged team members to improve by just the smallest margin—1 percent. But in five skill areas, this would produce a team that was 50 percent better. The team thought that they could improve 1 percent in each area.

What happened? The 1986-87 Lakers team is considered by many people to have been one of the greatest basketball teams ever. How did Pat do it? The same way Helen did—by negotiating a workable, manageable portion that almost guaranteed success.

I spent one summer teaching in Japan, where I marveled that a nation nearly annihilated more than fifty years ago is a wealthy, leading industrial power today. Many people have given in-depth reasons for Japan's rise to power, but one factor in particular merits consideration. The Japanese, who are convinced that producing high-quality goods is ultimately less expensive, are also committed to *constant* quality improvement—what they call *kaizen*. This concept is foreign to many people living in the West who don't think about quality, let alone how to constantly improve it.

One day my family visited the town of Omiya where Japan's bonsai masters live. These masters, who tend tiny little trees and shrubs that may be as much as 600 years old, have handed down their skills from family member to family member through generations.

I watched one man work in the presence of his grandfather—a bonsai master—and make minuscule adjustments to tiny trees worth thousands of dollars apiece. He knew that the tiniest refinements will eventually make an enormous difference.

Just as refocusing on quality improvement is important in keeping nations competitive in world economic markets and in pruning tiny trees, it's vital to us if we are going to advance on a personal level.

To help you gain this competitive edge, I've created a little response device to help you. I've also given it a Japanese-sounding name to stimulate you in your quest for personal development in godliness. I call it GISI-DICI, and this is what it stands for:

Gradual Improvement, Steady Improvement

Daily Improvement, Constant Improvement

It's my conviction that what most people lack is not intelligence but a workable approach that will help them put into practice what they already possess. GISI-DICI will give you the basis for reasonable change that you can expect to make. Your improvement will be gradual, steady, daily, and constant.

Let's suppose I just met someone who is discouraged, has given up finding a job, and no longer cares about looking attractive. I could say, "Get your life into shape," and walk away. And if I did that, the person might have reason to be discouraged and think, *What does he mean? And how am I to accomplish that?*

But if I walk up to that same person and say, "You know, you'd have greater success in finding a job if you dress better, comb your hair, and brush your teeth," and then give him or her practical ways to improve a resume and methods of contacting potential employers, I've helped the person take responsible, concrete actions. And these actions can be completed successfully because the person can chew on manageable bites.

As you respond differently and excitedly to the challenges that God brings into your life, your entire life experience will change. And not only will your life change, your family and friends will see the vitality and power in your life as you boldly face life's challenges. You will encourage other people, helping them to know that they can face difficulties successfully day by day and step by step.

May God bless you as you step out in faith, not content to just exist but taking charge so that never again will your life charge out of control. God has already given you *everything* you need to receive an abundant life and develop godliness. All you have to do is use it.

PAUSE FOR REFLECTION

1. Reread each of the A.N.S.W.E.R. steps. Now list personal difficulties in which you can apply these—starting today.

_____

_____

_____

2. Do you believe that trusting God is an important part of your relationship with God? Why or why not? Share an illustration from your life if you wish.

_____

_____

_____

3. Do you find yourself calling other people before you talk to God about a difficult situation? Why or why not?

_____

_____

_____

4. List six nonnegotiable beliefs to which you will cling.

_____

_____

_____

5. In which area(s) do you tend to blame other people and/or circumstances when you face difficulties?

_____

_____

_____

What are you going to do about that?

_____

6. List three areas in which you can apply GISI-DICI.

_____

_____

_____

7. What will you do in each of these areas?

_____

_____

_____

Take Responsibility for Your Life

Even seemingly insignificant actions lead to significant outcomes. Deliberately choose not to wait for someone or something to change you or your circumstances. Take responsibility for your life, beginning today.

As a young child, I found that my most difficult moments each day occurred just after I opened my eyes in the morning. I would lie in my warm bed knowing that I had to get up and dreading it. So I'd put it off, experiencing moment after moment of dread until my mother or father forced me to get up and get dressed.

I'm sure many of you can resonate with this simple childhood dilemma. In fact, the military wake-up song "Reveille" contains these words: "You can't get 'em up. / You can't get 'em up. / You can't get 'em up in the morning. / You can't get 'em up. / You can't get 'em up. / You can't get 'em up at all." Unfortunately, I lived out those words for many years, getting up only after torturously debating with myself about the merits of doing so.

Looking back, I realize that if I had gotten up quickly, I would have experienced little, if any, dread and accomplished more with less pressure. The solution was so simple. I just needed to *take action*. As a human being, I had been created to act, not to be a passive blob. Obviously I had to get up in the morning and get on with my responsibilities, no matter what.

When you start taking charge of your life, a seemingly insignificant but responsible action can lead to a significant outcome. Most people would not, for example, imagine that hopping out of bed right away in the morning rather than waiting desperately for a reason to want to do so is really a big deal. But it is. Such seemingly insignificant decisions and resultant actions affect many aspects of your life, from the way you get out of bed to your perspectives on the activities of a given day, to the way in which you live out the 86,400 seconds of that day.

Yet literally millions of people in the United States alone virtually wait for the state and federal governments to care for them. These people cannot even comprehend that they are responsible for their lives, even though recent welfare reform is forcing them to face that truth.

This unwillingness to accept personal responsibility isn't just prevalent in the United States. In fact, it's an even greater problem in Eastern Europe. The media has highlighted the great business and evangelistic opportunities over there, but a real problem has also surfaced. Millions of Eastern Europeans don't have a clue about taking personal initiative. For so many years, they were given jobs, apartments, and other benefits and services. Now a number of the people still sit around waiting to be told what to do.

When I worked with a mission group in Moscow, one mission worker had completed all the required forms that particular week. The paperwork revealed that he had visited everyone, followed up all his visits, and kept detailed records. But the director of the mission became suspicious, telephoned people who supposedly had been contacted, and discovered that none of them had been visited.

Challenged to explain the false claims he had made, the worker readily confessed them without remorse. "You gave me the forms," he said, "and I filled them all out just as you wanted. Everything was in place. What more was necessary?" Having lived and worked under communism, he had learned that the actual work didn't matter as long as all the forms were in order. He had no concept of taking personal initiative or responsibly pursuing his career. And on a larger scale, he certainly hadn't realized the importance of taking responsibility for his life.

Many other people, in contrast, want to accept responsibility for their lives but experience no meaning or purpose. So they drift along trying various things. Yet they remain unfocused, hungering for a reason to live and longing for responsibilities that will make a difference to something or someone—including themselves.

Recently I spoke with a native Canadian who grew up on a Native American reservation. Kim (not her real name) described how virtually every young person on the reservation was involved in a drug-filled, alcohol-filled, sex-filled lifestyle and then added, "But they aren't having fun." Their lifestyle seemed to them to be all they had and would ever have until they died. So many of them didn't care if death happened sooner than later. Without a biblical worldview, they had no sense that their lives mattered. They couldn't imagine projecting themselves into a vantage point from which they could see any meaning or purpose in their lives. Consequently, a high percentage of them committed suicide, never having experienced the hope of a future in which they took charge of their lives.

But Kim had chosen to become a Christian, and her entire life had changed dramatically. She discovered that her life mattered, that what she did and thought mattered, and that decisions she made would have eternal significance for her and other people with whom she would have contact. With God's help, Kim took steps to take charge of her life. Gradually those steps became easier and more confident, and she received the joy that comes from accepting personal responsibility and getting to know God in a personal way.

What is disturbing, if not as readily apparent, is that many people in North America are responding like the young people in Kim's community. They eat and breathe, but see that they make no lasting impact. They wait for something significant and positive to happen, but it seldom, if ever, does—at least not the positive things. And many of these people wander aimlessly or deliberately into death without any sense of meaning or purpose.

It's no secret that scholastic performance in many North American schools has deteriorated. Many pupils no longer believe that they have to work hard and make something of themselves. *Why do all that?* they reason. *We'll get by, or the government will take care of us if we can't make it on our own.* Or they simply live for today and don't think much about tomorrow.

Likewise, many adults haven't a clue as to what to strive for because they don't have a clue about what is worth living for. They have a deep spiritual void in their lives. Unlike previous generations of adults, they no longer think about or even recognize biblical absolutes. If the subject does come up, they receive it with the intolerance they once felt that an absolutes-dominated society demonstrated toward them. Because our culture has moved away from biblical absolutes and toward changing cultural norms, there is now no cultural rest or safety. Unborn babies are slaughtered, damaged people are truly endangered, and the wicked and violent are often given all the benefits and protections that righteous people deserve.

In a society such as ours that often discards everything of value, including other people, it's hard for individuals to think about commitment and take it seriously. Think of the cultural forces that subtly or blatantly encourage you not to face your difficulties with commitment. Think of the rationalizations that encourage you to blame others for your situation. In order to reach your God-given potential, however, you must be committed to facing your difficulties. The P.A.T. and A.N.S.W.E.R. tools will help you do that.

A movie titled *Sleepless in Seattle* focused on a fatalistic Greek sense of destiny. In this film the characters had no control over the romance of life. To a large extent, they waited until something "magic" happened. Sad to say, though, I think the movie became popular because many people are so miserable. They want something magical to happen but don't want to work to make it happen.

This is one reason so many marriages end up in divorce and never provide the romance that people so hungrily seek. Think about it. Most couples feel deeply in love when they consider marriage, but they haven't yet learned the principles that make a relationship continue after the "magic" seems to have worn off. These principles demand effort, initiative, and work. Yet before entering marriage, more and more people are requiring signed contracts designed to help them get out of those marriages. Are these men and women willing to accept responsibility for their weaknesses? Are they willing to keep commitments in order to take charge of their lives?

Consider, too, the number of people today who accept the best-paying jobs, not the best jobs in which they could really accomplish more, learn more, and fulfill a higher spiritual calling. With dismay my daughter reported the speech the career counselor gave to students in her high school. Speaking about the future, he said, "I wanted a good-paying job because I wanted all the toys." All too often greed, selfishness, and jealous ambition dominate a person's choice of career. So it's not surprising that many young people today lack a sense of calling or vision.

In contrast, if we were to interview a number of people who live out their spiritual callings in ways that make a difference, we'd discover people who take action—even significant risks—to fulfill God's calling on their lives. Notice what they do:

• They don't just wait around until the right careers open up. They make things happen.

• They don't wait for people to affirm their significance so they can start to feel good about themselves. They recognize their significance and identity before God and forge ahead in His strength.

• They don't just lie around wishing things could be different. They use their God-given abilities and talents to live out their faith.

GOD CALLS YOU TO TAKE ACTION

When I was on the staff of a psychiatric department, one of the most common problems we faced was a ward full of people who would not get up in the morning. Did this mean that they *could* not get up? Of course not! They simply chose to sleep away each day. No amount of psychotherapy, investigation, or insight could get them to get out of bed—until a staff member discovered their aversion to icy water being poured on them.

It was amazing how quickly this simple act changed their attitude about getting up. They were capable of taking action, and they did so because of a simple truism. They hated cold water far more than they hated getting up and facing the day. I can't recall a single patient staying in bed after being drenched or a single patient who had to be drenched twice.

START TODAY

The action of starting is fundamental. None of us can ever do anything with our lives if we don't take that first step. The apostle Paul put this idea into spiritual perspective when he wrote, "I press on toward the goal to win the prize for which God has called me heavenward in Christ Jesus" (Philippians 3:14).

God has given each of us the ability to "press on" from wherever we are in life. And this means that we don't have to be "pressed upon." The difference between the two is the difference between someone who is free and someone who sees himself or herself as a slave. Each of us can always choose to take action, even during the most unpleasant circumstances. We become imprisoned, however, when we believe that other people have control over us, and this belief can develop even when we seem to be the most free.

Some of us continue to blame other people in our past for the way we are today. Yes, each of us has been influenced by many factors, including relationships with people who did not always treat us the way we thought we should be treated. But we must not allow our view of ourselves to continue to be shaped by what others have thought of us— or how they still think of us. We must learn from the past and go forward with the Holy Spirit's help. We must challenge our false beliefs.

Some of us believe that a higher level of economic prosperity will make us free. But when we develop that kind of thinking, we have already become enslaved to the false idea that freedom consists in how many assets we have or don't have. Don't get me wrong. I'm not promoting poverty. I'm only emphasizing that true freedom breaks through the barriers of economic dependence. That is why Paul could write these words: "I know what it is to be in need, and I know what it is to have plenty. I have learned the secret of being content in any and every situation, whether well fed or hungry, whether living in plenty or in want" (Philippians 4:12).

Many of us have failed to learn that we are not at the mercy of economic trends or the whims of our employers. We are free to determine how we'll respond and must accept responsibility for the outcomes. We are not puppets. Psychologist B. F. Skinner wanted modern men and women to see themselves as just animals that can be easily conditioned by stimulus-response techniques. But we have the power to choose and are responsible before God for what we do with what we have been given. Our genetics do not ultimately cause our behavior. We are free to change any patterns of response—including those we have pursued all of our lives.

My brother clearly illustrates this freeing truth. About twenty years ago he became a Christian after leading a dissolute life. Shortly after experiencing God's healing forgiveness and gaining new purpose and direction, he knew that he needed to get serious about employment. He realized that he needed to take responsible action. He needed to take simple, basic steps that would get him moving in the right direction. So he filled out job applications and agreed to take a job with an agency in New York that transported disabled people. He agreed to do the work even though it only paid minimum wage.

Before he started this new job, he was offered another job selling potato chips for a significantly higher wage. Although he was torn between the choices, he chose to drive the disabled people because he believed it could be a ministry and that it was important for him to honor the commitment he had made to accept that job.

Soon his employer asked him to line up contracts with hospitals and nursing homes. Since he would no longer be a driver and was being asked to consider a new position, my brother realized that he should consider career options. He saw that he could do this new sales job on his own. Although it involved risk, there was a huge market for what he could offer, and he was ready to try it.

Within a few years he owned about forty vans, had sixty employees, and had the opportunity to significantly minister to other people. Several years later, while he was in the process of selling his business, I talked with him about his options. He had two serious offers. The first person was willing to pay hundreds of thousands of dollars more than the second, yet my brother sold his business to the second person. Why? The first buyer wanted to consolidate his business with another one in the city and thus remove most of my brother's employees from the payroll. The second buyer wanted to keep all of the employees.

"I'm responsible for the financial well-being of sixty people and their families," my brother said to me. "I can't just take the higher price if it means that they'll lose their jobs."

As my brother discovered, your first step isn't realizing that you can have an impact on your world. Your first step lies in realizing that you can have an impact on yourself.

Furthermore, most of the so-called "big" changes just *seem* big. In reality, these changes are really the results of many small, successive, and responsible changes.

With God's help, you can make new choices and change your circumstances—one step at a time.

PAUSE FOR REFLECTION

1. Describe a time in your life when you took a series of small, purposeful steps in order to accomplish a goal. What happened?

_____

_____

_____

2. What really gives you a sense of meaning and purpose in your life? Be honest!

_____

_____

_____

3. Why is the Bible such a key foundation in Christians' lives today?

_____

_____

_____

_____

4. Have you ever blamed other people and/or circumstances when something in your life didn't go well? If so, when?

_____

_____

_____

5. Why do you think it's easier to blame other people and situations rather than accepting personal responsibility and making changes with God's help?

_____

_____

_____

6. Why is it often hard to take the first step in a positive direction? What reason(s) do you give for not taking action?

_____

_____

_____

5

The Benefits
of Self-Control

God calls you to exercise self-control—a fruit of the Spirit.

I speak with Christians all over the world, and most of them would give almost anything to get their lives under control. It's not that they are doing all sorts of rotten things. It's just that they can't seem to put on the brakes and find out which way to go in order to make necessary changes and take charge of their lives. Pulled in different directions, they move in about every direction except the direction they really want to go—the one God encourages them to pursue. And some of these wonderful people ask me, "Aren't we supposed to give up control and let God be in control?" They seemingly want to make God completely responsible for everything they do and think.

In contrast, millions of people seek to completely control their own lives, their own destinies. Since the days of Adam, Eve, and Cain, people have been trying to be like God. Remember the poem "Invictus" by Henley with its proud boast, "I am the master of my fate, the captain of my soul"? That's clearly not the kind of control I'll urge you to adopt in your life. As Christians, we are not to strive for autonomy, to become the creators of our own laws and standards.

Although many people try, we cannot successfully create our own standards and legal system. We have been created in God's image according to His laws. We must not become laws unto ourselves, with each of us "doing what is right in our own eyes." (See Proverbs 3:7;

26:12.) Yet I'm sure you know many people who reject scriptural truth, seek to run their own lives, and try to create their own standards and values.

At the same time, however, this does not mean that we Christians are not supposed to exercise legitimate control over our lives. In fact, more often than not, not being in control is a common excuse for letting ourselves stay out of control. Haven't you noticed that in yourself? Let me explain this truth further.

Sarah came to me for help in as medicated a condition as anyone I'd ever met. She had lost her job, received disability benefits, and was in danger of losing her children. She wanted drugs and doctors to take care of her. So it was difficult for her when I said that she wasn't disabled and that at some point she would have to take charge of her life—now or after she had lost everything.

"I know," she said quietly, "but I'm tired and lonely and scared."

How often we allow fatigue, loneliness, fear, anger, and other emotional and physical factors to dictate and destroy our lives, all the while hoping that someone or something will turn everything around for us without us having to do a thing. Meanwhile, as in Sarah's case, who we are and what we have slips away from us.

If you and I are not taking charge of our lives—and that includes our inner lives (our thoughts, attitudes, and intentions)—then we are allowing other circumstances, influences, and/or people out there to take charge of us rather than taking control of our lives through the power of the Holy Spirit. But God wants you and me to take charge of our lives right now!

Perhaps you face an apparently impossible situation. No matter how bad things seem, the Bible teaches that you already have everything you need to fulfill your responsibilities. In fact, I believe the Bible mandates that you are, in the right sense, to take charge of your life and exercise self-control.

Listen again to what the apostle Peter wrote: "His divine power has given us *everything* we need for life and godliness" (2 Peter 1:3, italics added). That's an amazing statement, isn't it?

DESTRUCTIVE EXCUSES

Through the years Christians have told me, "Well, I don't have that fruit" or "I don't have self-control yet." But they were really saying, "I'm waiting to be zapped. I want something outside of me to change me."

Do you say things like that sometimes? All of us use similar excuses when what God calls us to do seems a little beyond what we are ready and willing to do.

Solomon, the wisest person who ever lived, offered this interesting observation: "Like a city whose walls are broken down is a man who lacks self-control" (Proverbs 25:28). The more literal Hebrew translation is, "He that rules not over his own spirit is like a broken-down city."

We are to rule over ourselves, to exercise self-control. By using the word *ruach*, which means "spirit," Solomon was clearly describing not only our inner person but our external behaviors.

When you meet a person who says, "My problem is anger," he or she is really saying, "I'm telling you now that I'm the kind of person who has no self-control. Please don't expect me to use self-control with you because I don't use it with anyone. And I get away with doing this because I tell people I'm not accountable because I don't have self-control."

Well, you could respond to this person by saying, "You mean you are like a city with walls that are completely broken down?" You see, we are to rule. Behind God's concept of self-control lie the concepts of mastery and rule.

God wants you to use all that you are and all that you possess to begin the take-charge process. Consider 1 Corinthians 9:24-27, where Paul wrote:

> Do you not know that in a race all the runners run, but only one gets the prize? Run in such a way as to get the prize. Everyone who competes in the games goes into strict training. They do it to get a crown that will not last; but we do it to get a crown that will last forever. Therefore I do not run like a man running aimlessly; I do not fight like a man beating the air. No, I beat my body and

make it my slave so that after I have preached to others, I myself
will not be disqualified for the prize.

When I'm running in a race, I need to keep focused on the course.
If I start running backwards or in circles or in a completely different
direction from the other runners because I feel like going that way,
what will happen? Clearly I won't win the race, and I'll end up wasting time and energy going in the wrong directions.

Paul, however, kept his focus. He controlled himself in every way
so that he wouldn't lose sight of the goal, so that he wouldn't lose sight
of the crown that he was pursuing, so that he wouldn't be disqualified.
This approach of Paul's, I suggest, marked all the physical and inner
dimensions of his life.

Look at Paul's intense preoccupation with taking charge of his life,
with exercising self-control. If you studied the Greek word translated
"self-control" for many years and delved into its deepest meaning, do
you know what you'd come up with? It simply means the control of
self. Paul dedicated himself to exercising self-control in all areas of his
life so that his life would not be aimless, so that his efforts would not
be wasted but would find their mark, so that he would not be turned
away from the direction God wanted him to go. He didn't want to run
aimlessly through life.

Don't you want to live a purposeful life? It's waiting for you.

YOUR JOB DESCRIPTION

God calls each of us to evidence the fruit of the Spirit. Paul wrote in
Galatians 5:22-23, "The fruit of the Spirit is love, joy, peace,
patience, kindness, goodness, faithfulness, gentleness and self-control. Against such things there is no law." Most of us have heard the
fruit mentioned many times. But did you notice that self-control is
mentioned last? I believe this is so because self-control is involved
in every fruit preceding it. When we've mastered self-control, we
will have the ability to be gentle and kind. Difficult challenges won't
keep us from expressing goodness, patience, and the other fruit of the

Spirit. After all, how can we be patient if we are not controlling ourselves?

But all of this fruit is part of a package deal. All the options come together. We don't have to pay extra for them. We don't have to wait for a second zapping from God, or a third. The fruit becomes ours when each of us chooses a personal relationship with Christ. The fruit of the Spirit may not blossom at the beginning. (Fruit takes time to develop.) But the fruit is still there because the Holy Spirit who produces it lives within us. We do possess everything necessary for godliness in life. All people who "live by the Spirit" possess this fruit. But we have to "put to death" sinful habits and attitudes that produce the opposite of the fruit of the Spirit.

WHY WE CAN TAKE CHARGE OF OUR LIVES

Many of us think, *I can't take charge of my life. That's only something the giants in the faith can do.* But saintly people who strive to know and obey God will tell you that they also face struggles in the area of self-control.

Paul got right to the point concerning which of us can take charge of our lives. After mentioning the fruit of the Spirit, he wrote, *"Those who belong to Christ Jesus* have crucified the sinful nature with its passions and desires. Since we live by the Spirit, let us keep in step with the Spirit"* (Galatians 5:24-25, italics added).

Did you notice the important truth here? Look at these verses again. Those of us who "belong to Christ Jesus" can take charge of our lives because we have crucified the sinful nature with its passions and desires. Through Jesus Christ, our sinful nature is dead. It no longer controls us. Our lives no longer have to be filled with sin. Because of what Christ did for us through His crucifixion and resurrection, we are freed from the bondage of sin. Each day we can choose to receive God's help to crush the things that cause us to lose control, that keep us from evidencing the fruit of the Spirit. Through God's power, we can exercise control over the little things in our lives and the bigger ones, too!

But why don't more of us experience this freedom in Christ? Why don't more of us take charge of our lives and "crucify the sinful nature" that enslaves us? What keeps us from giving up our sinful passions and desires and replacing them with self-control and the other fruit of the Spirit? If the answer were simple and easy, we wouldn't need to attend seminars, read books, and continue to draw close to God through Bible study and prayer.

Part of the answer is simple, however. Many of us as Christians don't realize that God calls us to take charge. He calls us to action. He doesn't want us to wait passively for something to happen to us. He calls you and me to realize that we must take charge—and that He has given us the power to do it!

In the next chapter, we're going to consider the value of discipline in becoming the person you know God wants you to become.

PAUSE FOR REFLECTION

1. In which area(s) of your life do you especially need self-control right now?

_____

_____

_____

2. Do you allow circumstances, influences, and/or people to direct your life rather than taking control of your life through the Holy Spirit's power? If so, how might you begin to exercise control today?

_____

_____

_____

3. Which excuses have you found yourself using to avoid exercising self-control in those areas? Be honest.

_____

_____

_____

4. What is keeping you from putting the sins in your life to death and running the best race and fighting the best fight you can?

_____

_____

_____

5. How can you, as Paul expressed, "Run in such a way as to get the prize"?

_____

_____

_____

To which "prize" do you believe Paul was referring?

_____

_____

_____

6

Discipline:
A Valuable Process

As you pursue discipline in your life, you will receive many lasting benefits. But the process will be painful as you choose which goals you really want to achieve, as you break barriers that used to slow you down or stop you altogether from reaching those goals, and as you receive God's correction. Will the results be worth it? You bet!

Emil Zatopek won three Olympic gold medals during the 1952 Olympic games—in the 5,000-meter race, 10,000-meter race, and the marathon. His former rival in the marathon, Perry of Great Britain, narrated the highlights of that race in a television documentary. He described how Zatopek finally reached him at the twenty-mile mark known as "the wall," the place where greatness and presumed greatness are easily separated.

Zatopek asked with his Czechoslovakian accent, "Perry, ze pace . . . too fast?"

Knowing that Zatopek had only raced a few marathons, Perry decided to thoroughly discourage him. He imitated Zatopek's accent: "Zatopek . . . ze pace . . . too slow!"

"Zank you, Perry," Zatopek answered, innocently looking him in the eye. Zatopek then surged ahead, never looking back.

During a post-race interview, Zatopek was asked, "Have you trained a full four years for these Olympic games?"

He looked at the interviewer incredulously and responded, "A full four years? I have trained a full fourteen years."

Zatopek had learned that in order to become an Olympic medalist, disciplined training was absolutely necessary. No matter how much it hurt, he had determined to keep at it until he achieved his goal. His gold medals were merely the result of countless steps.

Why did he do all that work for a race? Winning the race was his goal!

DISCIPLINE YOURSELF TO PURSUE YOUR GOAL

I know that you know the necessity for discipline, which is a byproduct of self-control. The apostle Paul clearly spelled out its importance when he wrote, "Discipline yourself for the purpose of godliness" (1 Timothy 4:7, NASB).

I also know that you know that holiness, achieved through the work of the Holy Spirit in cooperation with our faith and self-discipline, must be pursued. God, through the writer of Hebrews, told us to "make every effort . . . to be holy; without holiness no one will see the Lord" (Hebrews 12:14).

And I know that you know that in order to become the person God wants you to be, you must devote all your energy and effort to reaching that goal. It requires committed, goal-directed discipline. If you really want to accomplish something, it takes effort—effort expended toward a specific goal over a period of time.

What are your goals? What discipline is required to reach them?

In order to reach these goals, you will have to live the moments of your life consistently moving in that direction. If you start moving in another direction, you won't attain your goals. You'll attain something else. Then you'll have many excuses as to why you never got to where you wanted to be or accomplished what you wanted to accomplish.

A person who spends time and energy on everything that crosses his or her path—even things that he or she doesn't want to do—is not disciplined. Such a person is simply involved in ceaseless activity, as we've already seen. Paul called this "running aimlessly" in 1 Corinthians 9:26.

A skilled athlete offers us a great picture of discipline. As Paul wrote in 1 Corinthians 9:25, "Everyone who competes in the games goes into strict training." The word translated "compete" conveys the meaning of agony and gives us new insight into the picture of discipline, competition, and the games that Paul described. We have to be willing to put up with pain as we take charge of our lives and make necessary changes that will enable us to exercise self-control and live in obedience to God.

Whatever your goals may be, you will have to apply training and discipline in order to reach them, just the way a skilled athlete does. The athlete has to choose a desired result and practice over and over again, perhaps thousands of times, until the execution of the task necessary to obtain that result becomes second nature and can practically be done in his or her sleep.

One of my daughters is an avid basketball player. I recently watched her sink more than a dozen foul shots in one game. How did she achieve this level of mastery? Part of the answer lies in hours and hours of practice. Also every night when she gets into bed, she takes a basketball with her and lies there for between ten and fifteen minutes shooting pretend baskets and using every hand and finger movement necessary to accomplish the desired result. When she closes her eyes, she watches the ball arc perfectly into the basket every time. Not bad for a junior high kid, huh?

I heard a story about Larry Bird, who played basketball for the Boston Celtics. Someone asked him to shoot at a basket and miss, but he had trained and disciplined himself so masterfully that he had to shoot many times before he could miss. That's the kind of discipline that will enable you to achieve skill, success, or mastery in an area of your life.

As Christians, we have much more to strive for than just the perishable rewards athletes receive. The apostle Paul wrote, in effect, "Whereas people go into strict training to get a crown that will not last, we ought to exert this effort to get a crown that will last forever" (1 Corinthians 9:25).

He reminded us that we, as Christians, should exercise self-control and vigorously discipline ourselves because the reward God promises us is infinitely greater than that which a victorious Olympic athlete obtains. We should even exercise more discipline than that athlete because the eternal crown we receive will endure.

Discipline has interesting byproducts. When you've learned discipline, it flows into other areas of your life. Once you master the skill of working through a problem to its conclusion or a task to its completion, you develop an ability to focus on problems in other important areas.

If you are not achieving your goals, take a look at the time you've spent moving toward them or away from them. Whatever your goals—becoming a great shortstop, playing the piano for huge audiences, graduating from medical school, serving in an inner-city clinic, rearing godly children—you'll need to spend time pursuing what you want to achieve.

THE POWER OF DIRECTED ENERGY PLUS TIME

A basic truth is always at work—old habits die hard. Consider your life. You've watched your habits. You've watered them. You've nurtured and pruned them. You've helped them blossom. But what if they've turned into weeds and you suddenly want to get rid of them? Many people find that's not easy to do. They want instant changes to take place in themselves without having to really work at it. I think that's why drugs are so popular. They offer people an instant surge, an instant change in their feelings, without requiring them to work on their problems.

When I think of the discipline and work required to produce a lasting change, I think of the old willow tree that recently blew over on our farm. We had to get rid of it, and we could only do so much with a chain saw. Then we had to hire a backhoe operator to remove the stump. He was amazed by the depth and strength of the root system and had a difficult time removing roots that had been embedded for so many years.

Likewise, bad habits we've built in the past (and still may love) are often difficult and painful to eliminate from our lives. That's one reason why diets are so hard to maintain. It's not that dieting people don't want to lose weight; it's that they love the food that causes them to gain weight in the first place—and they love the food more than being trim.

Here's another simple truth to consider: You will become more and more like the things to which you devote your time. If you are a couch potato, don't assume that watching Arnold Schwarzenegger movies will transform your physique. That will require weight training, a proper diet, and other lifestyle changes. If you want to become a scholar of the Bible, you won't achieve that by reading newspapers two hours a day and spending five minutes a day in the Scriptures.

If you are committed to a particular goal, you have to spend time achieving it, and other activities will by necessity have to drop out of your schedule. In other words, you will experience some pain or loss as you apply discipline to your life and no longer choose to do certain things. But these losses are inconsequential when they are weighed against the gain you'll achieve. This is all part of the discipline process.

Perhaps you are thinking, *I have no discipline.* But even though I probably haven't met you personally, I know that's simply not true. If you are thinking this, you're giving yourself false information. I say this because such thinking conveys that you have no discipline required to strive toward your goals. The truth is, you have great discipline required to pursue other activities, perhaps even unfruitful or unbiblical ones.

It seems ironic, but it takes discipline to be ungodly, too. It requires the wrong kinds of discipline and the wrong commitments. A couch potato who doesn't exercise is not undisciplined; he or she has just learned to discipline himself or herself to sit on the couch and watch television for extended periods of time rather than being physically active and productive.

RESPONDING TO PAIN

God reminds us that "no discipline seems pleasant at the time" (Hebrews 12:11). The process of training to become more and more godly is difficult. It goes against our natural sinful tendencies. Although God's discipline doesn't seem pleasant, "later on, however, it produces a harvest of righteousness and peace" (Hebrews 12:11). But notice this added qualification: "for those who have been trained by it."

I don't like pain, and you'll probably admit the same thing. Pain is not pleasant. But we don't have to focus on the pain. When we "run with perseverance the race [life] marked out for us" (Hebrews 12:1), we have two choices. We can focus on the pain that we feel as we start training, become discouraged, and possibly stop running altogether. Or we can focus on the fact that we've started running, concentrate on where we are going and why we're going there and how far we've already come, and keep going in God's strength.

Through the years, coaches have urged their athletes to "focus on the gain, not the pain." Often this phrase is shortened to "no pain, no gain." And even though physical pain can, in reality, signal that our bodies need attention, this phrase continues to be popular.

Real success and mastery in athletics or any other area requires us to go beyond past limitations, to extend ourselves further than we ever have before, to focus on the result and break barriers that used to slow us down or even stop us.

Do you see how this metaphor of a race applies to you and me? As you discipline yourself and pursue your goals with God's help, you will surge past old barriers and move ahead. Although the process is painful, I tell people in my seminars that it results in "a good pain." It's not the kind of pain that leads to serious injury or death if it is allowed to continue. It's the kind of pain that leads to strengthening, to living life the way God intends it to be lived.

Have you ever spoken to a friend who did something wrong and then chose to make things right? I have faced this many times in my counseling practice. As the counselee shared what had taken place, I have said something to the effect, "I'm glad you got that worked out. How do you feel now?"

Often he or she has answered, "I'm glad I did make things right, but it really . . . hurts."

It isn't pain that's the real issue. It's how you choose to respond to the pain. Will you allow pain to stop you from taking charge of your life? Will you focus on the pain and decide that change isn't worth it because you are experiencing tension, conflict, or the pain of what you've done. Will you allow the pain to stand in the way of something you want to achieve?

It's easy to look at other people and say, "Hey, they've got it made. They don't have trouble with this. Why should I try?" But maybe those people had to go through the same struggles you face. Maybe they have battled with a particular sin, faced incredible illness, had to change careers, or nearly lost their marriages.

As you begin taking charge of your life and using discipline to overcome barriers that you've never gone through before, you can view the good pain you experience in a positive light. It isn't enough to want new positive changes in your life. You have to exercise discipline and strive to reach the results you desire. Discipline, in the deepest sense, involves the molding and perfecting of your mind and behavior—the internal and external aspects of your life.

In fact, strange as this may seem, the presence of "good pain" is a positive thing. God teaches us to "endure hardship as discipline" (Hebrews 12:7). To persevere in discipline is to be steadfast in the face of hardship. Hardship is something you encounter that you must see through, knowing there will be deliverance. It is a reminder that during such difficulty there is instruction and even nurture, which is why God revealed, through the writer of Hebrews, "'Do not make light of the Lord's discipline, and do not lose heart when he rebukes you, because the Lord disciplines those he loves, and he punishes everyone he accepts as a son'" (Hebrews 12:5-6).

THE VITAL ROLE OF CORRECTION

The word *correction* usually has a negative connotation. ("If you do this, you'll be corrected.") But is correction really negative? Isn't correction of a wrong good? If a teacher only marks a child's answers to a math quiz with the word "no" or "wrong," is that a correction? No, correction involves something very basic—marking what is wrong *and* communicating what is right. So the person who receives correction has the opportunity to learn something important.

A parent who understands what true correction really is will not only say to his or her child, "No, that's wrong; don't do that." The parent will also say, "This is what you can do," or "Here's why doing this would be better." Likewise, when God corrects us, He teaches us what is right.

The people whom God loves will face difficulties. The love of God is a key belief for Christians, and the writer of Hebrews linked God's love to discipline. We are to treat the hardship that comes into our lives as discipline, as training.

Why? A little later we read, "God disciplines us for our good, that we may share in his holiness" (Hebrews 12:10).

You see, the Lord corrects us, whom He loves. He will use everything He brings our way to develop godly character in you and me. His discipline will bear fruit.

But we can choose whether or not to receive His correction. In Proverbs 5 we read about a person who hated discipline and correction: "You will say, 'How I hated discipline! How my heart spurned correction'" (Proverbs 5:12). And that section concluded by showing the results of this kind of contempt: "'I have come to the brink of utter ruin'" (Proverbs 5:14). Hating God's discipline and correction leads to ultimate destruction—and to much trouble and sorrow on the way, as many people can attest.

But notice that this verse continues with these words: "in the midst of the whole assembly." In other words, the person who despises correction will receive public humiliation and disgrace.

In Proverbs we also read, "He who heeds discipline shows the way to life, but whoever ignores correction leads others astray" (Proverbs 10:17). When someone ignores correction and continues to commit sin, that refusal reveals a corrupt heart, a heart that will actually lead others to commit the very same error. Our errors—and our refusal to correct them—negatively impact other people.

Let me share a simple example. A parent who smokes two packs of cigarettes a day may have many rationalizations for doing so. He or she may say, "I tried to stop but couldn't," "I've cut back from three packs a day," or "I really don't need to give these up because two packs a day won't hurt me." But quite often the children who grow up in that home will model the mother or father and start smoking, or perhaps suffer ill health from secondhand smoke.

The same truth applies when people drink too much, commit immorality, become enraged at other people, gossip, lie on income tax forms, gamble, or commit other sins. You can take your pick and add things to this list. If you really care about what others who are important to you will do with their lives, you'd better model godly behavior for them. And you'd better not say, "I can't correct my behavior in this area." If you do, you are really communicating, "I won't do this." In God's strength, you can do what you have to do in order to pursue godly discipline.

If you learn from correction, it will enable you to show "the way to life" (Proverbs 10:17). The type of life described here is full . . . abundant . . . overflowing. Discipline and correction, when we learn from them, lead to a full, abundant life.

GOD WILL SHAPE YOUR LIFE

Slowly, but regularly and decisively, everyone who submits to godly correction discovers that God is molding his or her life, making it more perfect and righteous.

Let's say that you have lived an undisciplined life of error, sin, and carelessness for many years. If so, God offers you tremendous hope. Circumstances in your life may not change overnight, but as you take charge of your life and start making changes with God's help, you'll experience success in one area after another. That's what Ephesians 4:22 and Colossians 3:9-10 mean when they teach us to put off the "old self" and put on the "new self."

This new self is created to be like God and reflect true righteousness and holiness. Isn't that exciting! Godly discipline leads to a new self, which is molded after a new pattern. It's not the pattern of friends, family members, or other people around you. It's the pattern of God Himself, who is true righteousness and true holiness. But pursuing godly discipline and responding to God's correction will require everything that you have. You must be willing on every level of your being to exert and commit your energy, time, and efforts to being the person God has created you to be. And, in turn, you will receive the fruit of the Spirit, including joy.

When I was a young Christian, God was working in one area of my life after another. His correction seemed to come in waves, and I had to deal with it. At the time I was tempted to think that a godly, disciplined life meant a life of drudgery. But I was wrong. God showed me that fellowship with Christ, which comes as a result of the disciplined, obedient life of holiness, is the greatest joy. As I obeyed Him, even when I hurt and in spite of how I felt, God brought the delight of His presence to me as one area after another of pride and rebellion opened up and was surrendered to Him.

After Paul exhorted his readers to "strengthen your feeble arms and weak knees" (Hebrews 12:12), he then added, "Make level paths for your feet." Proverbs 4:26 foreshadows this truth. "Make level paths for your feet," Solomon wrote, "and take only ways that are firm." That is, we are not to become involved in evil. Then he added, "Do not swerve to the right or the left; keep your foot from evil" (Proverbs 4:27).

Ultimately, then, living a disciplined life will keep you from evil because you will have the strength and wisdom to avoid the snares that come your way. Also, as you seek what is true, noble, right, pure, lovely, admirable, excellent, and praiseworthy (Philippians 4:8), you will obtain a clear focus. You will obtain clear goals, which will keep you from swerving to the right or left. Is this process easy? No, but without discipline your life will be chaotic.

The Lord wants you to be changed. He wants you to be holy. Paul challenged his readers to offer themselves as "living sacrifices, holy and pleasing to God." He then added that this is the Christian's "spiritual act of worship" (Romans 12:1). You and I are to do this because of God's mercy toward us.

In the next verse, Paul revealed how to undertake this process, which introduces us to a pattern of nonconformist living. "Do not conform any longer to the pattern of this world, but be transformed by the *renewing of your mind*" (Romans 12:2, italics added). We are to live in nonconformity to the patterns of this world. Our minds are to be transformed to represent a pattern that opposes this world's lusts, greed, anger, and fleeting pleasures. Instead of conformity, there is to be "transformity."

The process of discipline is designed to remake us. Remember, everyone facing the battles of discipline knows that only the *results* of the struggles are seen in our behaviors. The contest has already taken place in our minds. What is won or lost in our minds, as we'll soon see, will determine what will be won or lost in our lives.

Are you living the kind of disciplined life that you know is taking you day by day and step by step in the direction you want to go? If not, you must begin to make changes now.

Choose the route of discipline, and you'll be blessed. "Whoever loves discipline loves knowledge," but whoever "hates correction is stupid" (Proverbs 12:1). God, Paul wrote, has given you "a spirit of power, of love and of self-discipline" (2 Timothy 1:7). This means that every area of your life will be different when your thinking in each area is changed.

You can be certain that as you progressively take charge of your life through the Holy Spirit's power, you will become more and more transformed into the image of Christ. And that, as a believer in Christ, is the top priority.

In the next section of this book, we'll explore the reality of God and how to apply it to our daily lives.

PAUSE FOR REFLECTION

1. List some of the goals you believe God is leading you toward.

_____

_____

_____

_____

_____

2. As you compare these goals to the ways in which you spend your time, what do you discover?

_____

_____

_____

_____

What changes do you need to make?

_____

_____

_____

3. In which area(s) of your life, with God's help, would you like to exhibit more discipline?

_____

_____

_____

_____

What steps are you willing to take, starting today, to begin to practice more discipline?

_____

_____

_____

4. Are any barriers standing between where you are now and where God wants you to be?

_____

_____

_____

_____

5. *Are you willing to receive God's correction so that you may share in His holiness? Why or why not?*

_____

_____

_____

_____

6. *How do you think God wants you to respond when He gives you a "correction"?*

_____

_____

_____

_____

PART TWO

Respond to Life's Challenges in Light of the Reality of God

Facing
Your Challenges

It's not what you face but how you face it that's impor-
tant. Ask the right questions, and develop a godly per-
spective. You'll be amazed at how much better you'll be
able to cope.

It's easy to forget that other people have faced struggles as tough or
even tougher than ours. They have also had to choose whether or not
to focus on enabling truths or disabling truths. And in many cases, their
choices determined the outcomes. To understand the importance of
focusing correctly, let's consider the difficult experiences of three people and how they chose to think about their circumstances.

JOSEPH: ABUSED, ENSLAVED, IMPRISONED

Remember what happened to Joseph, as recorded in the book of
Genesis? He faced a terrible situation. His brothers whom he adored,
loved, admired, and respected decided to kill him! But after Reuben,
the eldest brother, did some fast talking, they hurled him into a deep
cistern rather than killing him.

While in that cold, dark cistern, Joseph could hear his brothers eat-
ing their lunch, making jokes, and scheming his destruction. And then
he heard the sound of a caravan approaching, the traders' voices, and
his brothers agreeing to sell him for twenty shekels of silver.

Soon he was on his way to Egypt while his brothers finished their
lunch. Perhaps the last image he saw was that of his brothers holding

his multicolored coat—his most precious possession—the coat given to him as a token of his father's love.

We can picture Joseph a while later standing on the auction block in Egypt as the traders pinched his skin and looked at his fine-toned muscles. Ripped from his home and family, facing a lifetime of slavery, he still maintained hope.

"What was the good in Joseph's situation?" we might ask. "What gave him hope? He was an innocent victim of horrible treachery. Did he have anything left?"

Yes! Joseph was alive. As the ancient philosopher Cicero knew, "Where there is life there is hope." Joseph also had a strong faith in the character of God and chose to focus on the truth. He knew that he could depend on God.

Facing enormous emotional pain, virtually forgotten by his brothers, forced to enter a heathen culture, Joseph could have brooded on what had happened to him. He could have wondered what he had done to deserve such treatment and thought of himself as a powerless victim. He could have blamed himself and begun to believe that nothing he could do would get him out of his desperate situation. He could have allowed what his brothers did to him to lead him to despair and control the rest of his life through anger, bitterness, blame, and failure. Joseph could have just given up and pined away.

But he didn't. He could have nurtured the roots of anger and bitterness, feeding on revenge. But he didn't. Instead, he moved from his thoughts of pain to thoughts of hope, from disabling thoughts to enabling ones. Joseph made it a point to learn from what had happened to him and began using that knowledge at his first opportunity. He focused on the positives. He took charge of his thoughts, sought to obey God and draw near to Him, determined the godly direction to pursue, and walked righteously. Like Job, who stated, "I know that my Redeemer lives" after losing virtually everything but his life (Job 19:25), Joseph knew that God was working out His will and was trustworthy. Even when he was falsely accused and thrown into prison, he trusted God. In the end he became a top ruler in Egypt.

DAVID: THREATENED, PURSUED, FACING DESPAIR

As a young man, David faced tough challenges that included a murderous attack on his life, pursuit through the wilderness, hunger, loneliness, being cut off from the opportunity to worship God in the temple, and despair. As he wrestled with the fear that God had abandoned him, he wrote, "My tears have been my food day and night" (Psalm 42:3). This conveys a picture of tears dripping into his mouth—his only sustenance.

Facing despair, David chose to redirect his thoughts. Instead of focusing on his circumstances, he directed his thoughts toward God and asked two questions: "Why are you downcast, O my soul? Why so disturbed within me?" (Psalm 42:5). By the very act of asking these questions, David began to refocus away from his despair. And as he refocused, he began to rethink.

He didn't deny his present distress. This is an important truth to notice. He didn't say, "Wow, everything is great." He admitted that he was distressed and used the word *tsuris*, which means "to be cast down," "to be deeply disturbed," or "to be despairing." He also used the word *shochah*, which means "disquieted," "troubled," or "clamorous." His troubles were like a raging noise inside him.

We can picture him lying motionless on the ground in that darkened cave, crying out as he experienced deep emotional pain. He heard the echo of his despair bouncing off the walls. We could say that he faced deep depression.

What's significant, however, is that he refocused his thoughts. In the midst of hurt and pain, David didn't just think, *Everything is bad. Nothing will ever be good again. My life is ruined.* He shifted his focus from debilitating thoughts that were conquering him to questions that asked, in effect, *Are things really bad enough for me to become this downcast and disturbed?*

David experienced a battle of sensations—anger, despair, abandonment, fear—while hiding in the cave. But Saul wasn't standing in front of him at that moment. David wasn't actually fighting a physical battle with other soldiers. He was fighting a battle in his mind. And in the midst of that battle, he chose God and he found joy.

I am convinced that God has made it possible for each of us to be filled with joy, even in times of trial. Like David, we are capable of reminding ourselves of our blessings and of responding to our circumstances, other people, and God in ways that allow joy to infuse our lives. Christians who are always joyful are not born that way. They have learned to trust Christ in all situations. "I have learned to be content whatever the circumstances," wrote Paul, who then added, "I can do everything through him [Christ] who gives me strength" (Philippians 4:11, 13).

After declaring the reality of his despair, David declared the reality of God: "Put your hope in God, for I will yet praise him, my Savior and my God" (Psalm 42:5).

Matthew Henry, the Puritan, wrote this about Psalm 42: "If the Psalms be a mirror or a looking glass of pious and devout affections, this Psalm in particular kindles and excites such piety and devotion in us. Gracious desires are here strong and fervent. Gracious hopes, and fears, and joys, and sorrows are here struggling, but the pleasing passion comes off a conqueror."[1] What a concluding sentence! The "pleasing passion" (what we would today call joy or exultation) truly does conquer!

As David refocused his thinking, his thoughts and feelings changed. A very important truth emerges here. What matters is not so much the particular situation you are in but how you interpret and respond to it. For David, the critical thing to face was not his situation in that cave. It was, rather, how he understood his situation and how he interpreted it based on his understanding. And what he then did—how he chose to live—was based on that understanding and interpretation.

Inevitably how you live will be determined by how you interpret your circumstances—how you view them. Let's say that you are facing a tough situation. You may interpret it as a positive lesson and be happy about what you are learning. Someone very close to you may interpret your situation differently and be in great distress. Both of you responded differently based on different thoughts and interpretations.

Let's continue to look at David's situation. He used two questions to refocus: "Why are you downcast, O my soul? Why so disturbed within me?" (Psalm 42:5). Can you see the importance of asking questions like these—and answering them?

Notice that David didn't just ask *questions* when he was depressed. He asked the *right questions*. In effect, he asked this motivational question: "Why am I depressed?"

He could have asked, "I'm the anointed of God, so why do I deserve this kind of treatment?" He could have asked, "How can this be happening to me? Why am I alive? Is life worth living? What good is anything?" If he had asked those kinds of questions, he would have deepened his despair. But he asked the right questions, and they led to the renunciation of his depression. He chose to change his response to the terrible situation in which he found himself. He knew that he couldn't change his situation but that he did have the ability to take charge of his response!

What did David do next? He focused on the reality of God. He took an inventory of the blessings of God in the *midst* of his sufferings. "By day the Lord directs his love, at night his song is with me—a prayer to the God of my life" (Psalm 42:8). There was still something positive happening in David's life, and he focused on that.

There is tremendous power in positive thinking, just as there is tremendous power in negative thinking. The Bible offers us more than positive thinking. It offers us the positive reality of God. It enables us to focus our thoughts on the reality of absolute truth, not just wishful thinking. We can think positively because our thoughts are based on the character of God.

David wrote, in effect, "Your song is a prayer from me to you." On the basis of that positive truth, he was able to recognize that, although he *felt* abandoned, God remained with him. David realized that his feelings of abandonment would pass, and, because of that, he knew that God would lift him out of the pit of despair.

Finally, David faced the present difficulties and wrote again, "Put your hope in God" (Psalm 42:11). That became his command to himself for the present. Then he gave himself the reason: "for I will yet praise him, my Savior and my God."

Am I suggesting that simply asking the right questions will change your life? Of course not. But not asking the right questions during those times when they are necessary can be disastrous. Or asking the wrong questions can lead to despair and even physical death! Asking the right questions and giving yourself the right biblical answers based on who God is and what He has done for you can really—and quickly—get you started in the right direction, even if your actual circumstances don't change.

Everything depends on the quality of your questions and the truthfulness of your answers. I recently heard an account that illustrates this truth. During World War II millions of Jews perished in concentration camps. One Jewish man, however, refused to give up. After watching the slaughter of his family, he didn't ask, "How could something like this happen?" or "How did I get into a place like this?" Rather, he asked, "How can I get out?" And when the answer came to him, he placed his naked body among the distorted, tangled bodies of murdered Jews and was at day's end dumped outside the camp!

There are many examples of how asking the right questions led to the right answers and saved lives or changed the destiny of persons or nations. The crew of *Apollo 13*, for instance, was doomed to orbit in space endlessly unless NASA scientists could eliminate deadly carbon monoxide in the crew's quarters. They were hit with this incredible question: "Given the materials the astronauts have on board, how can a square pipe fit into a round hole?" The question demanded an answer, and if they had looked at its impossibility, they would not even have asked the question. But the right and only question led to an impossibly right answer—and the astronauts' lives were saved.

ALVIN YORK: ALONE, SURROUNDED BY ENEMY SOLDIERS AND DEAD FRIENDS

An example from World War I reveals again how important it is to face our challenges, ask the right questions, and focus our thoughts on the right answers.

Alvin York, a committed Christian, became a soldier during World War II after deep soul-searching before God. After just two weeks in battle, his regiment found itself in some of the bloodiest fighting of the war. He and the other Allied troops were surrounded by thirty machine gun nests. His battalion had been virtually wiped out, and he found himself in an exposed position at the bottom of a hill.

"Thousands of bullets kicked up dust all around me," he wrote. But he wasn't injured. He describes feeling "completely protected," certain he wouldn't be hit. *I can't hit any Germans while I'm lying down on the ground with everyone around me shot to pieces,* he thought. So he asked himself, *How can I possibly handle this situation?*

He answered his question by standing up. Using his rifle, he began shooting at the machine gunners. One by one, he silenced them, but his rifle became too hot to hold, and he was forced to drop it. At this point six Germans leaped out of a trench and ran toward him shooting. All he had was his six-shot pistol.

I'm in a terrible situation, he reasoned. He asked himself, *Do I know anything that will get me out of this?* Then he fired at the last man first, remembering turkey shoots back home. As he put it, "You see, we don't want the front ones to know that we were getting the back ones." He ended up shooting all six soldiers.

Completely demoralized, the remaining Germans were afraid to shoot for fear of revealing their positions. So York picked up his rifle and shouted for the entire German battalion to surrender. Then, as he put it, "I had the feeling that someone was shooting at me from behind. I turned and saw a German major standing behind me with an empty revolver in his hand. He had missed every time."

York commanded the major to call out all the nearby German troops and then asked him the easiest way back to the American lines. After he received directions, he departed in exactly the opposite direction, forcing the major to order more Germans to surrender along the way. So York returned to the American lines having shot 25 Germans and single-handedly capturing 132 more. Later he was given the French Legion of Honor and the Congressional Medal of Honor.[2]

How did York live through that situation and accomplish so much? Of course God protected him. Of course God was a shield about him. And of course he could have responded, "I'm overwhelmed, I am in despair, and I surrender." But he didn't. He asked the right questions. Although the difficult answers required bravery and courage, acting on them saved his life. Based upon the answers, he stood up, did what in hindsight looked impossible, and received unparalleled honor for his actions.

What else did York do? He didn't allow his fears or hesitations to dominate or stop him. He acted decisively. He took charge, and in so doing won a decisive battle single-handedly.

Today you have a similar choice! You may not have to stand up alone against hostile soldiers, but day in and day out you are called to stand up against the fears, anxieties, and despair of life. It's not what you face but how you handle it that's critical.

Can you think of anything that should ever be allowed to keep you from "standing up?" Through God's grace, you are enabled to take charge of everything that would hurl you down. By His grace, He empowers you to stand up and be the person He wants you to be!

If you have not used your mind properly, God will redirect and stimulate it. If you have abused your mind, God will heal and renew it. If you have not yet learned how to discipline your mind, God will empower you to do it.

The "secret" of trusting Christ is open to everyone. You are capable of taking every situation in your life and representing it in a way that will lead to joy or to despair. The interpretation is in your hands.

PAUSE FOR REFLECTION

1. If you were Joseph, how do you think you'd have responded to being on the auction block?

---

2. What was the secret of David's ability to handle all the suffering that came his way through no fault of his own?

---

3. Read Genesis 50:15-21. What do the last few verses reveal about Joseph?

_____

_____

_____

About God's work in your life?

_____

_____

_____

4. In Psalm 42:5 David wrote about hope in God. What does it really mean to place hope in God?

_____

_____

_____

5. What questions might you ask in order to correctly interpret a difficult situation in your life?

_____

_____

_____

8

The Power of Your Beliefs

What you believe influences what you will think, and what you think influences what you will do. So it's vital that you determine your core beliefs.

What you believe is key to how you will live life. What you believe heavily influences your ability to take charge of your life. When you pursue right beliefs that are rooted in Scripture and the character of God, you will experience blessing and joy. When you pursue wrong beliefs, not only will you do what's wrong, but you'll also be miserable or at least will create negative consequences.

Many people cannot articulate what they believe, even though what they believe affects everything they think and do. Other people try to articulate their beliefs and may or may not do so accurately.

Some people, for example, claim to be "*un*believers." They believe that nothing in the world grounds them and are in fact proud of it! They believe that nothing can be believed, and yet they believe their unbelief is true.

Some people believe in chance. "Randomness, nothingness, meaninglessness, and its concomitant hopelessness rule all of life," they say. Yet supporters of this philosophy actually embrace and communicate this belief to others with evangelistic passion.

Some people believe in luck. Although this belief system isn't much different from a belief system built on chance, the behaviors connected with it are often quite different. "If only I get lucky," a proponent of this belief system may say, "everything will be different."

Proponents of this belief system hate to admit that they must completely relinquish responsibility for the joys or sorrows in their lives. They believe that some new possession, situation, or relationship will change their luck. So they slave for a new car, home, or promotion, thinking that such things will secure happiness.

Unfortunately, even a wrong belief system can empower people to take action. The beliefs of Buddhists allowed them to burn their bodies during the Vietnam War. The beliefs of the Nazis allowed them to kill millions of Jews during World War II. Racist beliefs enabled plantation owners to enslave Africans in North America.

TWO BELIEFS, TWO RESPONSES

Not long ago, Al (not his real name) came to me for help. He exuded rage and told me that he hated God. "I'm like this," he stated, "because my brother was killed in an accident, and at almost the same time my mother died from cancer. It's God's fault. He's responsible. He did this to me. He could have stopped all this from happening."

Another man I'll name Phil held a different set of beliefs. "My four children were killed in a devastating accident," he said, describing the torment of his grief. "God has encouraged me in the midst of all this. I'm a believer, and my children were believers. God has encouraged me, reminding me that we'll all be reunited in heaven. I have something to hope for. This life isn't all there is." And from that time onward, he committed his life unswervingly to the service of God.

Let's think about this. These men, each facing a tragedy, had two completely different responses based on two completely different belief systems. You see, the events themselves didn't create the different responses; the men's basic beliefs concerning the events did. Al's and Phil's basic beliefs about life and death determined how they faced, interpreted, understood, and lived with their tragic circumstances.

If you, like Al, believe that life is meaningless and God is evil, your core beliefs will lead to a set of thoughts and actions completely different from those of a person who believes that his or her life is governed by a loving, personal, perfectly good Creator. Your beliefs determine the focus, passion, and significance you attach to who you are and what you do.

Perhaps you are familiar with Victor Frankl, an Austrian psychiatrist who wrote a book titled *Man's Search for Meaning*. He and his family were taken to Auschwitz, a German concentration camp. There the Nazis killed his family and many other people he loved. Yet he worked hard to encourage people in the camp who had lost all hope. As he watched them dying from perpetual loss and the tragedy of the situation as well as the physical rigors, he would tell them that they needed to have meaning in their lives. They had to believe in something.

One woman listened to him and attached meaning to a branch that she saw through the bars of her cell in the barracks. Other people attached meaning to different kinds of things. Not surprisingly, many of these Jews lived through the horrors of Auschwitz. But the survivors still faced difficult times. Following their liberation, many of the people discovered that the things to which they had attached meaning—a husband, a wife, a child, a parent, a friend, a hometown, a building, a job they hoped to return to—were not there. People had vanished. Cities had been destroyed. In some instances, virtually everything from the survivors' past was completely gone.

What happened to the survivors? Some of them experienced even more grief after their release from Auschwitz than they had experienced in the camp. Why? Because what really matters is not just believing in anything. What really matters is *what* you believe in. If a belief is false, it will eventually break down, taking the person who believes down with it.

CHOOSE BELIEFS BUILT ON THE FOUNDATION OF THE BIBLE

I have met and observed thousands of Christians. Regardless of their creeds, denominations, or theological viewpoints, they have shared a core of between seven and ten beliefs that strongly influenced how they lived their lives. The problem is, many Christians know that they hold certain core beliefs but don't pay much attention to them. These people, who do not consciously use their beliefs to help them understand and triumph over life's difficulties, are floundering in the sea of life. It's as if they know there's a life raft nearby but won't climb into it.

In the rest of this chapter, let's focus on eight core biblical beliefs to which you can consciously anchor your life. You can use these beliefs with ease during your daily activities. When you consciously embrace them, or similar ones built on your relationship with God and His Word, you will be taking a giant step toward changing your thoughts, attitudes, and behaviors. I'm not suggesting that your behaviors will be the last to change. I'm just saying that as your beliefs become more focused and influential in your life, many behaviors you have tried unsuccessfully to change will begin to change through the empowering work of the Holy Spirit.

I have listed the following core beliefs after counseling thousands of people, studying the Bible, and gaining life experiences. Feel free to build on these beliefs, rephrase them, or add some of your own. Entire books have been written on each of these core beliefs, I'm sure, but these few paragraphs will remind you of key truths that will help you take charge of your life and apply God's truth.

Belief #1: The Bible is the inspired, infallible, and inerrant
Word of God, and we must cling to its immutable truths.

This belief undergirds everything else I'll present to you in the rest of this book. I believe in an error-free Bible that cannot fail. "*All Scripture*," wrote Timothy, "is God-breathed and is useful for teaching, rebuking, correcting and training in righteousness, so that the man of God may be thoroughly equipped for every good work" (2 Timothy 3:16-17, italics added). As a Christian, everything you believe should flow out of your obedience to God's Word.

God has given us biblical truths to guide us. They impel us to love, pursue good deeds, and experience a life of abundant joy in the Lord. These truths can't be changed even if we change, and they remain true even if we no longer live by them. In the next several chapters, we will consider how to anchor our life changes to the Word of God.

Belief #2: We must become entirely new through Christ.

You and I must be entirely changed through a personal, ongoing relationship with Jesus Christ—not just challenged to change our behaviors, attitudes, and/or thoughts. We must accept Jesus Christ as our Savior and Lord, confess our sins, and be spiritually reborn. Paul wrote, "If anyone is in Christ, he is a new creation; the old has gone, the new has come!" (2 Corinthians 5:17).

Jesus emphasized this truth when he said to Nicodemus, "I tell you the truth, no one can see the kingdom of God unless he is born again" (John 3:3). Nothing could show more clearly the need for us to become totally different persons. We are to be spiritually born from above—from heaven, from the hand of God, by the Spirit of God—and are to be radically new and changed.

Without this radical spiritual rebirth in our lives, we can still change all kinds of thoughts, attitudes, and behaviors. People do that all the time, but such changes often do not last and are based on the wrong things, such as selfishness and self-protection.

The Pharisees, who are mentioned throughout the Gospels, illustrate what can happen when people who have not been spiritually reborn make moralistic changes. These religious leaders complained, for example, that Jesus spent time with sinners. "If you are really righteous," they told Him, in effect, "you'd only spend time with people like us." Their hearts were hard, and Jesus condemned them.

Belief #3: The Holy Spirit is the agent of change in our lives.

As a Christian, you have the Holy Spirit to help you and guide you into all truth about God. He is with you, even when you are struggling and feel as if you are completely on your own. He is your advocate with God the Father. He is the one the Father and the Son sent to convict, restore, and renew God's people. Unlike a non-Christian, you don't have to face troubles on your own. You don't have to change yourself through your own strength. The Holy Spirit, who knows which way to go in every situation, will guide you.

When Jesus was preparing to be crucified and return to heaven, the disciples were afraid. So Jesus comforted them by saying, "I will ask the Father, and he will give you another Counselor to be with you forever—the Spirit of truth. The world cannot accept him, because it neither sees him nor knows him. But you know him, for he lives with you and will be in you" (John 14:16-17).

As Christians, we can have an intimate relationship with the Holy Spirit. God is walking alongside us. He is our defender and helper as we determine to take charge of our lives.

Belief #4: God loves you.

Throughout the Bible we read about God's love, but perhaps it is captured best in John 3:16: "For God so loved the world that he gave his one and only Son, that whoever believes in him shall not perish but have eternal life." God sent His Son to redeem a people from out of the world to be His forever. What a wondrous truth! God's love should make you and me glad. It should make us thankful and fill us with gratitude.

There is nothing more foundational in our experience as believers than the love of God. When Christ comes to us and enters our lives, He is not a passive guest. He takes charge of our lives and enables us to take charge of all those areas that He wants us to bring into conformity with Himself. But what is most amazing is that He does it through love. If you belong to Him, He seeks to give you life, to teach you in your mind and heart. His mercies are new every morning.

One day a woman I'll name Francine came to me for counseling help. Her father had abused her for years, and although she had loved him, he had betrayed that love. To her a father meant someone who brought evil, pain, and betrayal. Gradually I helped her shift her focus onto the heavenly Father who *really* loves her. Accepting God's love wasn't easy for her, but she came to realize that God the Father could be more real, more significant, and closer to her than her earthly father ever could have been. This shift in focus gave her the opportunity to resolve her anger, pain, and torment through another relationship—one with her loving Father in heaven.

Belief #5: God controls all things—the good and the bad.

Years ago Rabbi Kushner wrote a best-selling book titled *When Bad Things Happen to Good People.* In this book, which dealt with God's sovereignty, Kushner concluded that God is sovereign over the good things that happen but has nothing to do with the bad things. I believe people bought the book because they were afraid of the reality that God is really sovereign over everything. But if He isn't sovereign over the difficulties and evil that occur in our lives, then who or what is? Chance? The devil?

The book of Job in the Bible is filled with trouble. Job, a good man, faced incredible suffering. When counselors came to him and saw that his children were dead, his fortune lost, and his body caked with oozing sores, they concluded in effect that Job must have been the most evil man on earth because they knew that God was sovereign. God would never have allowed such misfortune to befall a good man. The counselors had a pretty credible view of God's sovereignty, but they misapplied it to Job.

At the end of his terrible experiences, Job argued with God and received God's answer. It came upon him as a force from the foundations of the earth, asking, "Who is this that darkens my counsel with words without knowledge? Brace yourself like a man; I will question you, and you shall answer me. Where were you when I laid the earth's foundation? Tell me, if you understand" (Job 38:2-4).

God rained question after question upon Job until he answered, "I know that you can do all things; no plan of yours can be thwarted" (Job 42:2). Job spoke from his inner being with a certainty that would affect everything else he did during the remainder of his life. Having concluded that God was sovereign and could do all things, Job repented in dust and ashes because he knew that all the bad things that had happened to him were meant for good.

Thousands of years later, Paul wrote this to persecuted believers: "And we know that in all things God works for the good of those who love him, who have been called according to his purpose" (Romans 8:28). Notice these words. We know with certainty—not from mere speculation—that God causes all things to work together for good for those who love Him and have been called according to His purpose.

Who are these people who love God? Those "who have been called according to his purpose." You and I, as believers, have been called. As such, everything that happens to us works for good. Will God allow only good things to happen to us? No! He allows many things—good and bad, blessings and evils—to forge and build up our character and strengthen our minds so that we will follow Him with a sure faith regardless of external circumstances.

Jesus faced incredible difficulties—loneliness, scorn, scourging, nails being driven through his hands and feet, the burden of the world's sins—and yet He endured them. And He called us to trust in God's sovereignty, even though what we face is so minuscule in comparison.

Remember Joseph, whose brothers were going to kill him but decided instead to sell him to slave traders going to Egypt? Joseph spent many years in slavery, many of them in prison, for remaining righteous. Then Pharaoh promoted him to be second in command over all of Egypt.

Understandably, when Joseph's brothers realized who he was, they were terrified. But Joseph said, "Do not be distressed and do not be angry with yourselves for selling me here, because it was to save lives that God sent me ahead of you" (Genesis 45:5). He was stating the principle found in Romans 8:28—thousands of years earlier! God controls all things and will use even tragedies in ways we can't imagine in order to bring good and blessedness into people's lives.

Nothing is impossible with God that is consistent with His character. He is sovereign over all things. He controls all things. When you and I believe this, we can face anything that God allows to cross our path. And we will not only face it; we can grow spiritually as a result of it!

My friend's leg was smashed in a mountain-climbing accident. Rather than thinking that Satan was in control or that God didn't have a good plan for him, he believed that God would use his situation for good. In fact, since the accident, he has married the X-ray technician who cared for him at the time. My friend—like you and me—had a choice about what he would believe. What will you allow to shape you—the words of man or the words of God?

Belief #6: We must bear our cross daily.

Western Christianity, I believe, has largely failed to achieve significant impact because the central belief system of Christians is usually not well integrated into their daily lives. Belief in Jesus is not simply the acceptance of various doctrinal statements. Rather, when we believe that Jesus is our Lord and Savior, we are to live out the words of Jesus found in Luke 9:23-25: "If anyone would come after me, he must deny himself and take up his cross daily and follow me. For whoever wants to save his life will lose it, but whoever loses his life for me will save it. What good is it for a man to gain the whole world, and yet lose or forfeit his very self?"

Our lives are to be marked by denial of self, cross-bearing, and following Jesus. The crosses we bear are the afflictions we experience because of our identification with Christ. Seeing our difficulties in this light allows us to rejoice all the more because our fellowship with Him grows during difficult times of suffering.

Unfortunately, many of us do not experience joy in Christ because we believe that self should be exalted rather than denied. We have accepted the false belief that exaltation of self should take precedence over the rule of Christ. Consequently, our lives all too often reflect the rule of self, which means that elements of satanic tyranny control our lives and rob us of joy.

Belief #7: God calls us to model a living faith—
to live out our beliefs.

As we follow Christ, we are to model our lives after His—to learn what He is like and reflect more and more of Him in what we do and think. As we become more and more like Him, we will begin to enjoy the quality of life that no one and no troubles can spoil. We can live triumphantly even when we face physical death. Our beliefs will guide us, and our inner lives and outward behavior will become more and more fused in a life of service and devotion to Christ. Our self-concerns (even the best self-concerns) will no longer direct what we do. Then our faith will not simply be based on ideas that we separate from our daily activities. Our faith will be a *living faith*.

A number of Christians have separated what they say they believe about God from their daily lives. The results of this vary, but the most notable result is that such people don't seem to progress toward God and the quality of life He offers. They hope that their "belief" system will change them, but a dogmatic series of assumptions is not the same as living beliefs.

Some Christians ask, "Why do so many children of Christians forsake the beliefs of their parents?" I believe that this occurs because the children see a *disparity* what their parents say they believe and the actions that should normally flow out of having such beliefs. This disparity communicates that their parents really do not believe what they say they believe. The children recognize that inconsistent gap, know there is no vibrant spiritual dynamic in their parents' lives, and turn away.

Some parents try to instill certain beliefs in their children to keep them away from drugs, premarital sex, and other sins. But that isn't the purpose of Christian beliefs. Their purpose is to enable the Spirit-filled life of Christ to flow out of our inner being, enabling us to glorify God and enjoy Him forever.

You see, the living beliefs that we Christians possess are the life-activating realities of God. These beliefs don't just guide us toward our goals. They are the power that enables us to achieve and accomplish those goals. They undergird our lives and allow us to live bravely and boldly. We can only be changed as we reject the fears that keep us from courageously moving into a life of godly faith—with determined abandon.

When children take Christian beliefs seriously, it can be disturbing for their parents. In our family we have tried to live faithfully according to our biblical beliefs, but this can be quite challenging. For example, shortly after her seventeenth birthday our oldest daughter said that she wanted to serve as a missionary in Africa that next summer. Soon Christian friends who learned of her desire began telling us why we shouldn't allow her to go and described terrible dangers she would face. My wife and I decided to allow her to go because everything we believed was dependent upon allowing her to live out her faith.

As it turned out, she did face dangers, but the Lord delivered her. Thus her faith was strengthened. And after graduation from college, she decided to do missionary work in Bangkok. Again various warnings surfaced. Again we had to ask, "Is our faith big enough to trust God with our daughter's life no matter what might happen?" Again we supported her decision, and she learned personally that acting on her faith doesn't preclude the possibility of danger but that she can trust the Lord in dangerous situations.

Belief #8: We must face the beliefs that limit us—
and change them.

Just as we must live out certain beliefs in order to be empowered in fulfilling life's commitments, there are also certain beliefs that will limit us. All sorts of things that we allow to rule and dominate our lives are nothing more than self-imposed limitations to which we tenaciously cling. These can include, but certainly are not limited to, negative and destructive beliefs about who God is, about what He will do to and through us, about our gifts and talents, and so on.

Beliefs that limit our lives, our walk with the Lord, and our relationships with other people must be—and can be—changed. There is no reason for us to hang onto beliefs that keep us from becoming the men and women God wants us to be. We need to be willing to cast aside false beliefs we may have held all our lives and allow biblical beliefs that are true and right to dominate and direct our lives.

You want to make changes in your life, right? The Word of God must play a vital role in those changes. It will equip you to do what God calls you to do. So let's explore in more depth how you can anchor these changes to Scripture. What a difference that will make in your life! The issue is not what you have or don't have. The issue is, will you use what God has given you?

PAUSE FOR REFLECTION

1. What is the primary source of your core beliefs?

_____

_____

_____

_____

To what degree are they built on the foundation of Scripture?

_____

_____

_____

2. How do your core beliefs influence the way you think?

_____

_____

_____

_____

The way you feel?

_____

_____

_____

The way you respond?

_____

_____

_____

3. In what ways have your core beliefs influenced the way you responded to a recent problem?

_____

_____

_____

4. Which of the eight core beliefs are easy for you to apply? Why?

_____

_____

_____

Which ones are harder to apply?

_____

_____

_____

5. Describe a time when God used a difficult situation in your life to bless you or another person.

_____

_____

_____

9

Anchor Your Life Changes to God's Truth

When you want to make changes in your life, look first to the Word of God. Be confident that it contains the answers you need!

After I spoke at a seminar, a woman approached me. "Okay," she said, "I've thought about what you said. I believe my core beliefs are important. And I'm trying to bring those beliefs into line with what the Bible says. But it's so hard to do. It seems as if what I want to believe doesn't fit with what my emotions are telling me. I need something to help me deal with my practical everyday situations."

She got right to the bottom line. You see, when we want to make changes in our lives, we are to look first to the Word of God. It has the answers we need. It's our anchor point. But many of us have a huge problem—we lack confidence in the Bible. We don't really believe it's relevant to our lives today. Many pastors, for example, teach from the Bible but never guide their listeners in applying its truths. When I asked one pastor about this apparent oversight, he answered, "We're not supposed to do application. The seminary taught me that. And I heard it again when I took counseling courses."

He was really saying, "It's my job to simply teach people propositional truths that they can store up in their minds but not use in everyday life. The Word of God really doesn't apply to the practical realities of daily life." That perspective is false and so detrimental to people!

The Bible strongly and forcefully addresses this point. In 2 Timothy 3:16-17, which helped to anchor a core belief we examined in the last chapter, Paul wrote, "*All Scripture* is God-breathed and is useful for teaching, rebuking, correcting and training in righteousness, so that the man of God may be thoroughly equipped for every good work" (italics added).

Do you recognize this wonderful truth? *All Scripture* is breathed out of the mouth of God! Not just one verse. Not just one particular book. Not just the New Testament. Not just the Old Testament. *All of it*, and God has given it to you and me. Why? So that we may be equipped for, prepared for, adequate for every good work. The Scriptures equip us to be adequate in everything we have to do that is good.

In their efforts to find meaningful answers to important life-related questions, a number of Christians think, *What information do I need to know?* But finding the answers they seek is not a matter of *obtaining more information* on an intellectual level. Although it's important for us to know why we believe what we believe, the answers to every-day situations come by understanding *what God reveals to us* in His Word, absorbing it into our lives, and applying it. The Word of God is to be put into practice.

That's what Peter wrote about in 2 Peter 1:3: "His [God's] divine power has given us *everything* we need for life and godliness through our knowledge of him who called us by his own glory and goodness" (italics added). If we belong to Christ, we have everything we need right now! The issue is not what information we have or don't have. The issue is, will we use what God has already given us?

SET YOUR SIGHTS HIGH!

The Word of God is always before us, always above us, always giving us more to strive after. David wrote, "To all perfection I see a limit; but your commands are boundless" (Psalm 119:96). We can never reach the stage of perfection that is held out in the Word of God. Yet Jesus, in Matthew 5:48, encouraged us to set our sights high. "Be perfect, therefore," He said to His disciples, "as your heavenly Father is perfect."

One reason many Christians have so much trouble taking charge of their lives is that they set their sights too low. So they become mediocre

Christians. Mediocrity gets us only halfway to the goal. Mediocrity is an awful thing to settle for. But many of us still say, "I'm halfway there," or "I'm getting there slowly." (What we're really saying is, "I'm not willing to strive to get to the top, to know God in the most intimate way, to study His Word and apply it to my life every day.")

Not long ago I had the privilege of teaching at a Bible school in the Swiss Alps. The school wasn't just in the Alps, but it was located on the Matterhorn. Nancy and I hiked up a trail on the mountain, and we reached a spot where I thought we were on top of the world. The view was incredible, and I just wanted to stop and exult in our surroundings. I started to do that, until Nancy said, "Maybe we haven't reached the top."

Sweating, feeling too tired to go on, I answered, "How could we not have reached the top? Look where we are! This is where we stop."

"No," she replied. "Let's keep going. Maybe there's something beyond." We walked farther and realized that the real peak was some distance away. As the sun was setting, Nancy said, "Let's come back tomorrow."

The next day we walked several miles farther up a mountain path. We saw wild mountain goats, and beautiful flowers were growing out of the sides of the rocks. And then we reached the top—the real top— of the mountain. I felt as if I were going to be carried to the heavens. *What if I had stopped back there and never gone farther?* I thought. *I'd have missed all of this.*

Many Christians live their lives at a level that seems comfortable and may offer beauty. But they are missing something of great value because they haven't gone far enough in their walk with God.

You see, God has more in store for us than we can imagine. His boundless perfections await us. He has things just waiting beyond where we've traveled during our spiritual journeys. Sure it's great to be able to stop, look around, appreciate where we have come, and say, "God has certainly done a lot for me. Look at how far He has brought me." But God calls us to keep walking. He calls us, as Paul wrote, to "press on toward the goal to win the prize for which God has called me heavenward in Christ Jesus" (Philippians 3:14).

Whether a committed, disciplined runner is involved in the Olympics or a high school track meet, what is his or her goal? To run the best race possible and perhaps cross the finish line ahead of all the other competitors. But if the runner runs a great race for 99 percent of the distance and then decides to stop running, he or she won't finish the race.

Matt Biondi provides a perfect example. In the Seoul Olympics of 1988, he swam in seven events and won gold in five. What was interesting was the 100-meter butterfly event. Matt led all the way. But in the last two meters, he failed to take the last stroke and crash into the wall. He was beaten by Anthony Nesty of Surinam by a centimeter.

It's important for each of us as we run the spiritual race each day to learn how to run so that we can keep going from the beginning to the end. And that involves pressing on . . . reaching forward until the very end . . . not getting bogged down.

MAKE A DECISIVE COMMITMENT TO BIBLICAL PRINCIPLES

In order to take charge of your life and see changes occur, you must decisively commit yourself to implementing biblical principles. The Word of God challenges us to live outwardly as well as inwardly, and it offers us solutions to life's practical problems. The Bible shows us how to deal with anxiety and worry, envy and jealousy. It shows us how to face problems and suffering in biblical ways. It shows us how to deal with destructive habits.

• What's the answer to fear? "Perfect love drives out fear" (1 John 4:18).

• What's the answer to guilt? "If we confess our sins, he is faithful and just and will forgive us our sins and purify us from all unrighteousness" (1 John 1:9).

• What's the solution to conflict? The Bible teaches us to deal with the problem, not just with the person. Matthew 18, for example, urges us to try to be reconciled with someone who has sinned against us.

You can't just change yourself by your own power. Time won't change you much either. You need to allow God and the power of His

Word to change you. Change in your life will come as a result of your decisive commitment to God and obedience to His will for your life.

Suppose a person comes to me and says, "My marriage is rotten. I've seen it going downhill for years. I'm fed up with my spouse. . . ." He or she raves on and on.

No matter what shape that marriage is in, if that husband or wife is not willing to make changes that will show love and respect to the spouse, the marriage will not improve. Time alone won't make it better. Both partners must be willing to change—and be committed to applying biblical principles to their situation.

Let's consider a few Scriptures that communicate the necessity of decisive commitment:

• "Count yourselves dead to sin but alive to God in Christ Jesus. Therefore *do not let sin reign* in your mortal body so that you obey its evil desires" (Romans 6:11-12, italics added).

• "Offer your bodies as living sacrifices, holy and pleasing to God—this is your spiritual act of worship. *Do not conform any longer* to the pattern of this world, but be transformed by the renewing of your mind" (Romans 12:1-2, italics added).

Do you see the importance of decisive commitment? "Count yourselves dead to sin." "Do not let sin reign." "Offer your bodies as living sacrifices." "Do not conform any longer." Will you take these principles and apply them to your life? Will you study God's Word and apply it to your life?

NO EXCUSES!

Perhaps you are thinking, *I'd love to have the decisive commitment to make that change I need to make, but I don't really feel committed to making it. And because I know that I don't really feel committed, I can't make the commitment.*

It's an easy rationalization to make, isn't it?

Decisive commitment doesn't mean that you or I have to wait until we *feel* like changing. If we wait for that, we may wait a long time, because sin often feels good.

God doesn't say, "It feels bad to sin." He says that sin is wrong.

You and I need to make the changes we know are right—according to what the Bible says is right—whether we feel like it or not. If you are a believer in Jesus Christ, "the one who is in you is greater than the one who is in the world" (1 John 4:4). Remember, you have the power of the Holy Spirit at work in your life. The devil can't make you do anything, so he's not the one to blame.

You and I need to take responsibility for making a decisive commitment to implement biblical principles. We each need to confess our sins and seek to make necessary changes through the power of God and His Word—whether we *feel* like it or not.

When I speak to groups on this topic, invariably someone will say, "Richard, I hear what you are saying, but I don't want to be a hypocrite. I don't want to stop doing something just because it's wrong to do it and right to do something else. I want to be completely committed in heart and soul to doing what's right."

This sounds good, but it's really another excuse. If you wait until you are decisively committed to change before you start doing what's right, chances are that you won't do it. Doing something we don't want to do doesn't make us hypocrites. A hypocrite is someone who does something he or she doesn't want to do but says, "I wanted to do it."

Do you get the point here? Rather than saying, "I really want to do everything that I'm doing," the person says, "I want to do what God wants me to do whether or not I feel like doing it." In other words, decisive commitment will lead you to say, "My commitment to God is much stronger than my commitment to those things that give me sinful pleasure, so I'm giving up my sinful pleasure for the greater pleasure of doing what God wants me to do."

It's so easy to allow "feeling" words (or intellectual arguments) to keep us from taking the decisive actions that the Word of God commands. If you are a parent, you know that kids often do wrong things. Have you ever heard a parent say to a child, "I want you to *feel* like doing what I want you to do?" I never have. Instead, parents say, "I want you to do it!"

Every time we do something sinful, we've given in to what we've felt like doing instead of doing what God calls us to do. That's a consequence of being in a feeling-oriented, sinful society and a feeling-oriented, sinful world. No matter what we feel like doing, the Bible calls us to commit to obeying God and living according to His Word.

Joshua, a leader of the Israelites, assembled all the tribes of Israel at Shechem and challenged them to decisively commit themselves to God. "Now fear the Lord and serve him with all faithfulness," he said. "Throw away the gods your forefathers worshiped beyond the River and in Egypt, and serve the Lord. But if serving the Lord seems undesirable to you, then choose for yourselves this day whom you will serve. . . . But as for me and my household, we will serve the Lord" (Joshua 24:14-15).

That's the kind of commitment God calls us to make. That's the kind of commitment God calls us to live out, to demonstrate. We are to do what it takes to serve the Lord. We are to live righteously. We are to worship together on the Lord's Day. We are to worship as a family daily. We are to do things that please the Lord. We are to train our children in the way they should go, rewarding righteousness and punishing wrongdoing. We are to live according to His Word.

IT'S TIME TO DECIDE

Maybe you are excited about following God and applying His Word to your life. Maybe you are not. If you are not committed to becoming the person God wants you to become, why is that? What's the reason? Have you thought about what's standing in the way of your decisive commitment to Him?

It's easy for people to make excuses for not taking charge of their lives or making necessary changes. They say such things as, "I don't know if this will really mean anything anyway," "I'll do it but not right now," "I'm not sure this will work," "I really don't know if the Bible applies to *my* situation," and a host of other excuses.

What is keeping you from making a decisive commitment to change, with God's help? Are you too proud to admit that you are making excuses? Are you allowing your emotions to dictate which beliefs you'll cling to today? Through years of counseling with people, I've come up with two key reasons why people won't wholeheartedly commit themselves to God.

First, *they love their pet sins.* It's true that sin is pleasurable for a season. And many people today love to do what's wrong, are not concerned about God's judgment, and don't care about pleasing God. According to the Bible, such people are not children of God and thus lack the power and ability God could provide to bring about necessary changes in their lives. Are pet sins keeping you from making a decisive commitment, and yet you don't want to ask God's help in removing them from your life?

Second, *people feel as if they've failed and have given up trying.* Sometimes it's tough to persevere in the spiritual race of life. We feel like hiding in the bushes during a cross-country race, letting everyone else run a lap and then jumping back onto the course. (This happened to my daughter during a cross-country race in junior high school. Someone was planted in the woods to veer her in the wrong direction, since they knew she would be in the lead. She took the wrong path and went about .5 kilometer before realizing the treachery. She thought about giving up but decided to run it out anyway, even though she had to go an extra kilometer. She ended the race in seventh place, but her determination to finish was gold medal quality.)

Maybe we've run our hearts out in our own strength, not met the standard, and are just plain exhausted. Maybe we've actually accomplished quite a bit of progress but can only see how far we have yet to go.

Have you felt like giving up at one time or another? I think we all have. God understands that, stands by us, is willing to forgive us, and will run (or walk) beside us. "Call to me," says the Lord, "and I will answer you and tell you great and unsearchable things you do not know" (Jeremiah 33:3).

After giving His disciples the Great Commission, Jesus stated, "Surely I am with you always, to the very end of the age" (Matthew 28:20).

Many other verses, too, proclaim God's care and faithfulness, His forgiveness and mercy, His love and empowerment. He is waiting to come alongside you right now. Will you give Him that opportunity?

PAUSE FOR REFLECTION

If you are decisively committed to change, through the power of God and His Word, I urge you to complete the following action steps today. They will help you to align a specific change you'd like to make in your life with the Bible.

1. Determine a basic change in your life that you'd like to make. Following are several examples:

- "I'd like to make time to read the Bible and pray every day."
- "I'd like to seek forgiveness from my daughter."
- "I'd like to quit drinking alcohol when I return home from work."

_____

_____

_____

2. Using a concordance or other Scripture tools, find at least several Scriptures that deal with the particular change you'd like to make. Write them here:

_____

_____

_____

3. Now set a standard related to the change that is possible for you to reach—something attainable. Following are some examples:

- "To start, I'll read half a chapter of the New Testament every day and then pray."
- "I'll call my daughter and ask her if we can get together next week at a time that'll work for her."

• "On my way home, I won't stop at the liquor store anymore. And when I get home, I'll change my clothes and do some work on the house."

_____

_____

_____

4. Now pray and ask God to help you meet your commitment.

5. On a separate sheet of paper, write out a covenant between you and God in which you spell out your decisive commitment to start making that key change in your life. It might read something like this:

"I desire with all of my heart to please God, to do this for His pleasure and not my own. I am committed to [being a better _____, completing _____, crushing a particular sin, and so on], and I purpose that with the help of God, my Lord and Savior, I will _____."

6. Sign the commitment and tape it up someplace where you'll see it regularly until you have fulfilled the commitment.

7. Tell someone close to you about your decisive commitment to make that change and ask him or her to follow up on your progress toward your goal. It's important to be accountable to someone.

8. Read your covenant every day and change it as needed to keep up with your progress and the new changes you'd like to begin making.

9. Realize that change can take time and that it's better to start somewhere than never to start at all. Edith Schaeffer has used this expression: "If you want perfection or nothing, you're going to have nothing every time."

10. Pray every day that God will guide your thoughts, your words, and your actions and empower you to remain decisively committed to Him and to the goal(s) you've set for yourself.

10

When Thoughts or Circumstances Seem Overwhelming

When you feel that you are losing control, cling to the changeless character of God, who has proven His faithfulness.

The lines on Marcia's face spoke volumes. She knew the meaning of suffering and confusion. For years she had lived with an abusive man. She hadn't married him and could have left him at any time. Finally she did leave him, and soon after that she became a Christian. But she kept asking herself over and over, *How did I ever get myself into that situation with him?* She'd ask me, "Will I ever be free from all this guilt? I can't forgive myself."

Marcia was experiencing more than just regret and the consequences of her decision to live with that man. She was experiencing her sinfulness. When she wasn't a believer, she did not question her lifestyle and did not struggle with guilt. But after she met Christ, she became aware for the first time of the hideousness of her sins. As she looked at life with a biblical, moral perspective, she understandably wished that her problems had magically and instantly gone away as soon as she came to Christ. She wanted the consequences of her bad decisions to be erased. But that didn't happen.

She experienced profound disappointment in herself. She recognized the sinful decisions she had made—and sometimes still made.

She saw the things she had done that had not pleased God and the ways in which she still fell short. But after I shared with her the forgiveness that Christ provides, she discovered a level of peace and hope she'd never known.

Most of us can relate to Marcia's struggles. Even as Christians, we continue to act in ways that are contrary to God's ways, to think wrong thoughts, and to fail to meet the standards God sets before us in His Word. And we continue to experience difficult circumstances that don't disappear.

Maybe you feel disabled by a thought or circumstance over which you seem to have no control, and you feel helpless. Maybe an important relationship has ended. Maybe you've suffered a financial reversal. Maybe you've lost a job after many years of dedicated work. Maybe someone close to you has just been diagnosed with cancer. Only you know how heavy you feel inside. You may feel that whatever has happened to you is disastrous and permanent. Maybe you find yourself sinking deeper into depression, even despair. If this is your situation, you have a choice. I'll illustrate it using the example of two people in the same office who lose their jobs within several days.

One man says, "I'll never find another job. I'm too old. Who will hire me? It took me a while to find this job, and now I've got to find another one."

A coworker assesses her situation differently. "This is just the push I need to get a better job," she says. "God provided this job in the first place, and I really do need to work for a while longer. Even though I do have talent, ability, and experience, it may not be easy finding a job I like as much as this one. But God knows, and He has taken care of me up to this point. I'm sure He will keep doing it, in His timing."

The truth of the matter is, the man who views his situation as hopeless may be right. Maybe there are no jobs out there for him. Maybe he is too old. Maybe nobody will want him. But if there is a job opening, who do you think will get it? Will it be the person who says, "You probably don't want me. I was laid off my last job; I am not really capable, and I am too old"? Or will it be the person who has confidence in herself and is obediently asking God to direct her paths? (See Proverbs 3:5-6.)

The attitudes that you and I have toward our challenging circumstances—and the core beliefs backing them up—are so important. As Christians, we have even more going for us than the opportunity to choose positive attitudes. We have God standing with us! He is our refuge during times of trouble (Psalms 18:2; 46:1; 91:2). He hears us when we call to Him. He offers us a firm place on which to stand no matter how helpless we feel or how challenging our circumstances are.

CLING TO GOD—YOUR LIVING HOPE

King David, who lived during Old Testament times, knew what it was like to face trying circumstances. As we've seen, he battled depression. He had hunger pangs sometimes. He became tired of fleeing for his life through the countryside. He felt lonely. He felt angry. But through it all, he clung to certain key beliefs that undergirded his relationship with God.

He described those realities beautifully in Psalm 40:1-3: "I waited patiently for the Lord; he turned to me and heard my cry. He lifted me out of the slimy pit, out of the mud and mire; he set my feet on a rock and gave me a firm place to stand. He put a new song in my mouth, a hymn of praise to our God."

Remembering the great things that God had done for him, David knew that God would continue to lift him out of deep pits and set his feet on a firm place to stand. Marcia, on the other hand, had allowed past problems to drag her down and had taken her eyes off God. She had forgotten about His forgiveness and faithfulness and became consumed with her troubles.

Sad to say, I've met many people in evangelical churches throughout North America, Europe, and Asia who respond to their circumstances more like Marcia than like David. They feel helpless and trapped in the mire of life and can't seem to get out of it, even though God is willing to help them face their difficult challenges. They forget that all of their difficulties don't immediately leave as soon as they become Christians. They forget to think about all the great things that God has done for them. They forget that He is capable of lifting them out of the mire, setting their feet on a firm place, and establishing their way. They become consumed with their troubles and forget about God and His life-changing power.

The Psalms reflect life the way it really is. They reflect our trouble, our hope, our joy, and our sadness. They also reflect what happens when a person focuses on troubles rather than on the character of God. But the Psalms also teach us how to emerge from depressed, lethargic, anxious, and/or angry states and focus on important life-changing issues.

There's a big difference between positive thinkers who talk as if their feet are firmly planted on a rock, on one hand, and the "take-charge" approach of the Word of God that states that God is our Rock (2 Samuel 22:2; Psalm 89:26). The "positive" thinkers lack a spiritual foundation in their lives. They talk positively to themselves while they sink into quicksand. "I'm okay, you're okay," they tell themselves. "Things are getting better." But the quicksand comes closer to their mouths, noses, and eyes and finally covers them completely. Yet all too often we Christians think and talk as if we are in the quicksand while we're actually standing on the Rock!

It's one thing to be trapped in quicksand, struggling to survive. It's quite another to build our lives on the Rock and look back over our past. Yes, we can look back into the pain of what has occurred and, like Marcia, be transfixed by our sins. But, as Paul commanded, we are to forget what lies behind and strain toward what is ahead (Philippians 3:13).

When the psalmist faced a situation that brought him terrible torment (we don't know exactly what it was), he had to choose how to respond. Psalm 77:1-2 reveals his decision: "I cried out to God for help; I cried out to God to hear me. When I was in distress, I sought the Lord; at night I stretched out untiring hands and my soul refused to be comforted."

The psalmist also "thought about the former days, the years of long ago," and posed a number of questions in rapid-fire order. They so clearly reveal the focus of his mind. "Will the Lord reject [me] forever? Will he never show [me] his favor again? Has his unfailing love vanished [from me] forever? Has his promise failed [me] for all time? Has God forgotten to be merciful [to me]? Has he in anger withheld his compassion [from me]?" (Psalm 77:7-9). He focused on his calamity. He said in effect, "I don't see anything good in my present circumstances."

Can you relate? Have you felt like this? Have you experienced a situation in which nothing seems good? When everything seems to be wrong and confused? When doubts rise to choke you? That's what caused the psalmist to ask, "Has his unfailing love vanished [from me] forever?" The psalmist's calamity initially turned him into a foolish man who asked foolish questions. After all, what kind of unfailing love vanishes forever?

Believers throughout the ages have asked similar questions, which only lead toward one place—despair. If you or I come up with the belief that God has totally and permanently rejected us, where else can this belief lead us? If the one unchangeable person—and the unchangeable reality of His unchanging love for us—has completely and forever abandoned you and me, we are left with total despair. Why? Because His promises are our only hope in this life and the next. If in this life His promises will fail us, there is no hope.

Suddenly, however, the psalmist refocused his thinking. "Then I thought . . . ," he wrote. After asking questions that could have immediately hurled him into utter despair, he began to express clear, right-minded thinking. He realized that the way he had been thinking was absolutely foolish and only demonstrated his lack of good judgment and accurate thought. He then asked in effect, "What kinds of questions am I asking? To ask questions like these shows what's wrong with me, not what's wrong with God."

So the psalmist continued, "To this I will appeal: the years of the right hand of the Most High. I will remember the deeds of the Lord; yes, I will remember your miracles of long ago. I will meditate on all your works and consider all your mighty deeds" (Psalm 77:10-12). Another translation reads, "the full right hand of Him Most High, through years, must changeless be."[1]

Do you see what the psalmist did? He refocused on the changelessness of God. He remembered God's deeds and God's miracles that had taken place years earlier. Had the psalmist's situation changed? Absolutely not! Whatever had hurled him into anguish was still there, but his attitude had changed because he remembered the unchangeable reality in his life—God. Rather than dwelling on himself and his infirmity and reflecting that focus by asking additional foolish questions, he focused on God.

If, as the psalmist did, we choose to focus on the changelessness of God, we move mentally from our present distress to the eternity of God. What a move! Then we can echo what Paul wrote, "Our light and momentary troubles are achieving for us an eternal glory that far outweighs them all" (2 Corinthians 4:17). Which "light and momentary troubles" did he face? He was shipwrecked, beaten, stoned, left for dead, imprisoned, and ultimately beheaded. If these are "light and momentary," I'd like to know what some of the more difficult ones were!

Paul was saying in effect, "This is how I've come to view the afflictions in my life when I compare them to the eternality—the changelessness—of God. Everything that happens to me is temporary and superficial, and I don't even think it is worth comparing."

TRANSFORM YOUR MIND

An amazing change of perspective occurred in Paul's mind. That's why, when he wrote about the Christian life, he told us to be "transformed [metamorphosed] by the renewing" of our minds. Then he added, "you will be able to test and approve what God's will is—his good, pleasing and perfect will" (Romans 12:2).

Has your mind been renewed? Have you been transformed? The transformation of your life begins in your mind—in the way you think. The transformation is not a static quality in your mind; it's the way in which you use your mind. We've all been in situations in which we don't see God acting for what would seem to be our good. How will we choose to respond? In which direction will we focus our thoughts?

Do you use your mind the way the psalmist did at the beginning of Psalm 77 and ask foolish questions? Many people use their minds in this way much of the time. Or do you use your mind to focus on God's changeless character and on what He has done for you and other people?

When you and I cling to God's changeless character, we are able to look forward to the future without worrying. Instead of looking back at our sinful shortcomings the way Marcia did, we can look back to God's unfailing deeds. We can say, "I know God is at work. He has worked in the past. He doesn't change, and He will continue to work in my life."

When the Israelites crossed the Jordan River, they set up twelve stones as a memorial. Why did they do that? They wanted to look back, not to the miserable times they'd had in the wilderness, but to God and the fact that He had taken them from the wilderness into the Promised Land.

Do you grasp this point? *It's okay to look back; what matters is what we look back to.* The Israelites were not to look back and focus on their forty years of disobedience. They were to look back and focus on God—how He had delivered them from sinful disobedience and brought them into a land overflowing with milk and honey.

The psalmist needed to focus on what God had done for him because he did not see God acting to ease his present situation. Have you ever been in that place? I have. But the psalmist realized that if he remembered God's deeds of long ago—deeds that revealed His mercy, His love, His favor, His compassion, and other aspects of His unchanging character—then the truths he could reaffirm would see him through the crisis. Needing help in getting through the pain, the psalmist looked back at how God had expressed Himself in the past—His love, His mercy, His compassion, His grace. Although the psalmist wasn't experiencing God's visible work in his life, he nevertheless affirmed, "I know He is at work. He has done it in the past. He doesn't change. He's the same God."

The psalmist traced back thousands of years, recalling what God had done. And you know, what he recalled gave him hope in place of despair. He was not in a hopeless situation. He realized, as we all should, that to trust in God and be hopeless is a contradiction in terms.

This passage contains another important point. The psalmist wrote that he would appeal to "the years of the right hand of the Most High" (Psalm 77:10). In order to do that, though, he had to know the Scriptures. Likewise you and I need to know the Scriptures in order to remember what God has done for us.

Jesus strongly condemned the Sadducees, religious leaders of His day who had knowledge but didn't seek to know God, much less turn to Him for wisdom and guidance. "You do not know the Scriptures or the power of God," He said to them (Matthew 22:29). Consequently, they were not able to amass evidence for the powerful work of God.

The Word of God contains a mountain of evidence that can contradict whatever negative psychological states we may be in today or find ourselves in tomorrow—despair, anger, anxiety, loneliness, and so on. The evidence demands a verdict! But if we don't know the Scriptures, we'll not be able to amass the evidence for the faithfulness of God. The psalmist knew that the Scriptures showed that his present distress should not be the ultimate focus of his attention.

As we remember the deeds of the Lord, we'll remember that He loves us with an unfailing love (John 15:12; Romans 5:8; Ephesians 2:4-5). We'll remember what Jesus did for us at Calvary. We'll remember that God delivered His people from slavery. We'll remember the fullness of our redemption. We have, as Hebrews puts it, "something better" (Hebrews 11:40). So why do we remain in despair, confusion, anger, and/or anxiety? How can we justify remaining in those states when we have Jesus? We have the cross! We have the fullness of redemption!

EXERCISE YOUR MIND IN THE RIGHT DIRECTION

The psalmist then added, "I will meditate on all your works and consider all your mighty deeds" (Psalm 77:12). Now he was able to meditate on creation. He was able to meditate on the Flood. He was able to meditate on Abram leaving Ur of the Chaldeans to go to Canaan. He was able to mediate on the establishment of Israel. He was able to meditate on the Israelites' deliverance from slavery. He was able to meditate on the giving of the Law and the defeat of Israel's enemies. He was able to meditate on the establishment of the temple and the worship of God.

When we experience challenging, distressing times, we can choose to exercise our minds in the right direction or the wrong one. God has given us enough works so that we can meditate on them for a lifetime and not run out of material! He has given us truths that will give us comfort, encouragement, and hope. But like a weight lifter, we can't expect our muscles to grow stronger just because we place a set of weights in our room but never pick them up. Just having dumbbells in the room with us while we sleep won't make any difference. We have to exercise our bodies; we must exercise our minds, focusing on the changeless character of God.

Now notice where the psalmist moved next! From having doubtful questions about God, he progresses to sharing a testimony of faith and truth. "Your ways, O God, are holy," he wrote. "What god is so great as our God? You are the God who performs miracles; you display your power among the peoples. With your mighty arm you redeemed your people, the descendants of Jacob and Joseph" (Psalm 77:13-15).

Notice he didn't say, "Your ways, O God, are good," "I can accept Your ways," or "I'll bear with these things as long as I have to, but I hope I don't have to put up with them for long." He said, "Your ways, O God, are holy."

Having questioned whether God had removed His love eternally from him, the psalmist asked, "What god is so great as our God?" His rhetorical answer was, in effect, "No god is as great as my God, the God who redeems His people."

Do you see the transformation? Within just a few verses, this man shifted from despair and lostness to deliverance and redemption. Likewise if we want to break patterns of despair, fear, terror, and/or lostness, we need to focus on the work of Christ. When we focus on the redemptive work of Christ, we suddenly focus on salvation—the greatest event and ongoing work that has happened since time began. We focus on the greatest deed expressed by the character of God, an ultimate memorial to His mercy, grace, and love.

The psalmist then recounted how God had led His people through the waters of the Red Sea. "Your path led through the sea, your way through the mighty waters, though your footprints were not seen" (Psalm 77:19). The psalmist revealed that when we find ourselves in trouble, we're not to look around us and focus on the trouble. Doing that will cause us to become more depressed or experience other types of pain. Rather than living by sight, we are to live by faith—the same way the psalmist did, the same way the early Israelites did as they remembered God's works, including how He led them through the sea. God was with them, but He didn't leave a single footprint! The only evidence of His presence was that the entire nation had asked, "What's going to happen to us when the chariots reach us?" They had then crossed from one side of the Red Sea to the other through the parted waves. God took them through, and no one saw even a single footprint of His.

Finally the psalmist closed this psalm by writing, "You led your people like a flock by the hand of Moses and Aaron" (Psalm 77:20). Instead of continuing to question whether God would and could ever love him again for what he had done, the psalmist came to understand that God tenderly shepherds His flock.

There are strong parallels between the psalmist's situation and responses and our situations and responses today. The evidence we have of God working in our lives is our deliverance—the salvation we have in Christ. God delivers us through the cross of Christ. That is the centerpiece of life and joy. And when we learn to look to Him and away from our difficult situations, both past and present, we'll find the resources we need.

If you rest in the character of God, your life will be filled with so much good. You won't have to manufacture hope. You won't have to try to survive the challenges on your own. You won't have to depend on yourself or other people to get you through. You can depend on God, whose character never changes. And in His power you can take further steps and take charge of the life God has given you.

In spite of your past sins, your present situation, your current doubts, and your fears concerning the future, you can always focus on the evidence! God has saved you. But don't look for His footprints. In his letter to the Christians living in the northern part of Asia Minor,

Peter wrote, "Though you have not seen him [Christ], you love him; and even though you do not see him now, you believe in him and are filled with an inexpressible and glorious joy, for you are receiving the goal of your faith, the salvation of your souls" (1 Peter 1:8-9).

When you have learned to place your faith in Christ and trust in the character of God, you'll find the resources you need. You will not only make it through life, you will take charge of your life through His power and grace.

PAUSE FOR REFLECTION

1. Which thought or circumstance in your life is particularly troubling to you right now?

_____

_____

_____

2. How have you responded to it—with a positive or negative attitude? (Be honest.)

_____

_____

_____

3. As you think about this chapter, which aspects of God's unchanging character relate to this problem?

_____

_____

_____

What hope does His character give you?

_____

_____

4. David remembered what God had done for him when times got tough. What has God done for you?

_____

_____

_____

5. Why does being rooted in who God is and in the Bible offer a much stronger foundation than just positive thinking?

_____

_____

_____

6. What does Christ's sacrifice on the cross for you reveal about His love for you and His plan for your life?

_____

_____

_____

11

The Call to Godly Obedience

Instead of feeling powerless, avoiding pain, or blaming other people or circumstances when life is tough, strive to obey God. Become the person He calls you to be and receive His joy. Allow Him to use your challenges to achieve His will in your life and in the lives of other people.

I counsel people who have all kinds of problems. Invariably, they believe that if an unpleasant colleague or unfair boss were removed, if certain people would only do this or that, if a spouse would respond in more appropriate ways, then their own lives would greatly improve. But I propose that this type of thinking avoids the real issues.

How much good does it do, for example, for you and me to focus on what we believe other people's faults to be and blame them for how we are feeling? If we believe that our enjoyment of life is based on what *they* do, we are implying that they, not we, are responsible for the degree to which we experience quality of life. Do we really believe that we are simply the victims of other people's behavior? Or are we willing to work instead on ourselves—our attitudes, our weaknesses, our lack of love, and so on? We will always face relational and circumstantial difficulties, yet our enjoyment of life can and must continue in the midst of them.

The apostle Paul expressed a firm commitment to work on his life. "I beat my body," he wrote, "and make it my slave so that after I have preached to others, I myself will not be disqualified for the prize" (1 Corinthians 9:27), and again, "I have applied these things to myself" (1 Corinthians 4:6). He didn't take anything for granted, not even things about himself. He sought to do everything he could do to become a person who didn't try to gain heaven by presumption (as if that were possible) but by faith. He didn't doubt his salvation and wasn't trying to fight his way into heaven. But he was aware that a man or woman cannot take himself or herself for granted before God.

Rather than trying to straighten out everyone else first, Paul committed himself to straightening out his own life so that the path to which he called other people would be filled with righteousness and truth, not strewn with the debris of a wrecked life. And he sought to do this as a man changed and dominated by God, not by his emotions. He sought to live by grace through faith in Christ alone. And he did it by taking active steps toward God and being willing to live radically for Him.

TAKE THE FIRST STEP

As we saw in the last chapter, it's important for us to focus on the character of God and what He has done—and continues to do—for His people. But this is only part of the process. The other part involves our decision to take a positive first step—and then other steps. Taking that first step is vital. In fact, many people have moved out of severe depression just by beginning to do what had to be done!

God rules, empowers, and governs our universe, even though the earth is still in the bondage of sin. He also empowers us to be radically different from the moaning, grumbling, complaining individuals around us. We are called to be radically different from the kind of person who blames how he or she feels on someone else. We are called to be radically different from the kind of person who views himself or herself as powerless because the difficulties seem so overwhelming.

Paul clearly identified this kind of radically different person when he wrote, "I pray that you, being rooted and established in love, may have power, together with all the saints, to grasp how wide and long and high and deep is the love of Christ, and to know this love that surpasses knowledge—that you may be filled to the measure of all the fullness of God" (Ephesians 3:17-19). A few verses later, he wrote, "Put off your old self, which is being corrupted by its deceitful desires" and challenged his readers "to be made new in the attitude" of their minds (Ephesians 4:22-23).

If we consider these verses attentively, we understand that we are to be made *new* persons in Christ, with new attitudes that infuse our minds. This biblical truth teaches that a new Christian begins to exercise control when he (or she) lets God change his or her former attitudes and replace them with new godly ones.

Paul went on in the next few verses of Ephesians 4 to list radically new behaviors. Consider a few of them:

• "Put off falsehood and speak truthfully" (v. 25).

• "In your anger do not sin" (v. 26).

• "He who has been stealing must steal no longer, but must work, doing something useful with his own hands" (v. 28).

• "Do not let any unwholesome talk come out of your mouths, but only what is helpful for building others up according to their needs" (v. 29).

• "Get rid of all bitterness, rage and anger, brawling and slander, along with every form of malice" (v. 31).

• "Be kind and compassionate to one another, forgiving each other, just as in Christ God forgave you" (v. 32).

RECOGNIZE THE GOOD

When you and I live out who God has called us to be, our transformation will be so revolutionary that not only will we change, we'll effect positive changes in others. We will love, give, speak kindly, be gracious, and forgive. This is part of what it means to be empowered by Christ. We will also come to realize that no matter how challenging our situations may be, not only can they work for good in us, but they can work for good in other people.

Paul often challenged people to recognize the possibilities for good in difficult situations. But it wasn't Paul the armchair philosopher who waxed eloquent on such ideals. It was Paul the apostle who faced great adversity. He saw his dreams smashed, and as a result of the smashing, he saw greater dreams realized. His situation speaks clearly to us today.

Paul, we recall, always dreamed of going to Rome and spreading the Gospel in the heart of the Roman Empire. Always on the move, he enjoyed success as he traveled great distances while planting churches far and wide in Asia and Europe. He saw many new Christians glorifying God.

So how do you think Paul felt when, instead of Rome becoming his field of operations, he had to locate his headquarters in a small cell? And in case that cell wasn't enough to restrict his movements, two guards were assigned to be with him at all times! Perhaps he thought, *How can this be happening to me? How can God really be in control? How can any good come out of this?*

If you and I were to look at his situation simply in terms of how the circumstances appear, what other conclusions might we draw? But Paul didn't just view circumstances in terms of how they appeared. He knew that if God had narrowed his field of evangelistic endeavor from the whole city of Rome to a room with two soldiers who changed shifts every eight hours, then that was his mission field.

Instead of bemoaning his fate, Paul shared the grace of His Lord and Savior with the soldiers. Instead of longing for a way to escape his chains and cell, Paul used his opportunities to the fullest. In Philippians 4:22 not only did Paul greet his readers, but so did the saints in Caesar's household! Paul, who viewed his hardships as opportunities, revealed that palace officials were now followers of Jesus Christ.

It's easy to use our hardships as excuses to complain about being victims and to dwell in self-pity. But while imprisoned, Paul wrote four letters that have become some of the most important writings in history—the Epistles to the Ephesians, Philippians, Colossians, and Romans. Paul, who dreamed of starting a dozen churches in Rome, blessed countless people as a result of what could have seemed like a disaster to him. Just think what the world would be like without these four books!

Paul never allowed himself to assume that his life and ministry would be more blessed or improved when he was released from prison or that his external situation would improve in other ways. Rather than just wasting away in prison, he believed that his responsibility before God was to trust and obey Him in whatever situation he found himself. Consequently, because of his obedient attitude, untold millions of people have been helped during these last 2,000 years by the fruit of his prison labor.

CHOOSE GOD'S JOY

Why was Paul's life so spiritually fruitful? For one thing, he was dominated by real faith in the core of his being. He put aside everything that he had hoped to do and pursued God with all his strength and zeal. Instead of basing his level of enjoyment in life on circumstances or other people, Paul received great joy from God.

But how can we, like Paul, avoid being trapped in worry, depression, fear, or other negative states when we face difficulties? How can we receive the type of joy that he exhibited even when his circumstances were awful? How, in other words, can we move from a negative emotional state and stop hinging our emotions on other people and circumstances?

Years ago a movie titled *The Deer Hunter* was released. The main character was a prisoner of war in North Vietnam, and part of the plot revolved around the games of Russian roulette that the Vietnamese forced the American prisoners to play against each other. But after the war ended, the main character continued to play the game even though he didn't have to. Finally, his obsessive need to play ended in his death by a bullet from his own gun.

Why didn't he stop? I asked myself. *He could have stopped anytime.* It's easy for us to think that if we were placed in a similar situation, we'd stop playing. But you know, countless people continue to act out patterns that are killing them. For example, have you ever heard someone say, "I'm depressed," when he or she was really saying, "I don't have anything to do with this depression. It's just here. Where is it coming from?" The lives of such people are filled with pain. They live as if they are outsiders living in their bodies, as if what they do is beyond their control.

Many of us fall into this sinful trap, too. Instead of allowing God to transform our lives, we act as if we are powerless victims, who are simply pawns of other people and circumstances.

Some of you may remember a comedian named Flip Wilson, whose television persona, Geraldine Jones, was popular for many years. After doing something that was supposed to be "kind of" sinful, she would strut on the stage, look you in the eye, and say, "The devil made me do it."

Throughout your life you'll experience both good and bad situations. You can't control your external circumstances without basically going into protective seclusion, and even if you pursued that bizarre extreme, you'd still have to deal with despair, loneliness, isolation, and so on. As a human being, you can never avoid difficulties entirely. But here's a truth that will help you take charge of your life with God's help: You can choose how you'll respond to your experiences. You can create the emotional and mental states in which you choose to live.

Let's say that something sad happens to you or someone you love, and you experience grief for a while. That's quite different from choosing to be depressed for the next three years. You can make that same type of choice to be joyful.

Paul didn't write, "Catch the Spirit," "Catch the joy," or "Catch a joyful feeling when you are out of control." He wrote, "Rejoice in the Lord always. I will say it again: Rejoice!" (Philippians 4:4). He urged us to demonstrate that we are responsible individuals who choose to respond obediently to God, who commands us to actively rejoice no matter how challenging our situations may be.

DEPEND ON GOD WHEN YOU FACE PAIN

Every time you become angry, fearful, anxious, or depressed, that emotion has been triggered by something that affects the neurochemical pathway into your brain. Perhaps some thugs beat you up badly and said as they left, "We promise that we'll do worse things to you next time." And now you live in fear.

Maybe you studied hard for an examination in college but kept telling yourself, *Oh, I'm so stupid. I'm going to fail.* And now every time you enter a testing situation, your brain keeps associating it with anxiety and failure.

Maybe other children mistreated you, so you decided to prove to them that you have worth. And today you are still trying to prove your worth to other people by having the best job title and earning the most money you possibly can.

Maybe your parents didn't love you, and you habitually associate the belief, *I'm not loved,* with every important relationship in your life. So whenever something or someone reinforces that belief, it's as if a trigger pushes a button and plays songs to you that provide substantiating evidence that you are worthless and do not deserve love.

Maybe someone has hurt you deeply, and you wind up hating or avoiding everyone—not only the person who hurt you but other people who may hurt you. *That person is getting too close to me,* you may think. *He's going to hurt me, but I'll never let him get close enough to hurt me. I've learned my lesson.*

Maybe you are depressed, and instead of feeling miserable about yourself, you have become angry and think, *How dare these people treat me like this? I hate them for doing this to me.*

Ironically, people who respond in these or similar ways are choosing to hurt themselves. Can you see this? Do these people really want to hurt themselves? Do they want to do or think things that make their situations much worse? Of course not. Everything they do is designed to make themselves feel better! But all they end up seeing is their seeming worthlessness. Is it any wonder that people who respond like this do things that are self-destructive? Why do children physically or emotionally "run away" from home? They run away to feel better, to protect themselves.

In the '60s, many people smoked marijuana to feel better. Convinced that society was horrible, crass, and materialistic, they spent their hard-earned money and rolled marijuana cigarettes. Today many people do drugs like cocaine, in addition to marijuana, that provide immediate highs but destroy their lives. And because of the craving for drugs, addicts often commit crimes against innocent people.

In virtually any large city today, young girls are involved in prostitution. Quite often, wanting to feel better, they were drawn to people they thought would love them. Instead, those people have led them into a trail of degeneracy—and sometimes to death.

Why do young people—and adults—drink excessive amounts of alcohol? It makes them feel better at that moment. They choose to do something physically harmful and irresponsible just to feel a little better, even though they know they'll probably feel rotten later and are damaging their bodies. People often become dependent on someone or something in order to feel better.

I'd like to propose what may seem to be an unusual solution to these kinds of dependencies. I believe that the solution is to choose the right reality upon which to become dependent—God.

Today people often make statements such as these: "Don't be dependent!" "You are autonomous." "You're alone in the universe." "Rule your own life." "Choose to be number one." "Be your own best friend." The idea of dependency offends people. They don't like to think of themselves as being dependent, but they are! All of us by nature are dependent from birth. As we grow up, we still remain dependent on other people, at least to a degree.

Do you remember these lyrics in a song sung by Simon and Garfunkel: "I am a rock. I am an island. And a rock feels no pain. And an island never cries"? Which of us is really a rock? Which of us is really an island? Which of us doesn't cry—on the inside anyway? Yes, you can put up self-protective walls and seek to be independent, but the price you will pay is the loss of the capacity to feel—to experience pain, courage, fear, joy, and so on. You will become unable to receive the blessings God has in store for you. You will blame other people instead of focusing on trusting and obeying God.

But you can make a different choice because of who you are in Christ. Since God is changeless, loves you just the way you are, will forgive your sins, and sent His Son to redeem you, you can choose to make yourself dependent upon Him.

Why not reach out for God, who can truly help you, rather than seeking other people and things that will only cause you to feel better temporarily and ultimately hurt you and other people?

You have the opportunity, starting today, to choose an abundant life in God. Remember, apart from choosing God, every choice you make to find satisfaction on your own is a destructive way of trying to minimize or eliminate your pain. That's why counselors, psychiatrists, psychologists, and social workers are so busy. People continue to choose self-destructive ways of thinking and acting in order to feel happy, to feel good, to escape pain momentarily. Yet such ways create bigger, deeper, and far greater pain later on. Sometimes people even commit suicide because they have gotten themselves into such terribly deep pain by trying the wrong ways to feel good. Death appears to be the only way they will truly feel better.

As a Christian, you can choose to become dependent on God and to put aside sinful things that bring you temporary comfort. You can rejoice in the fact that one day you will be in heaven, where everyone will rejoice and be blessed forever. And God calls you to speak out and let people know that the physical end of this life isn't really the end. It's the beginning of an eternal state.

Feeling good isn't the final goal of mankind, even though many people, even many Christians, arrange their lives around that belief. Rather, we are called to glorify God and derive our well-being through Him.

Almost everyone today seeks loving relationships of one kind or another because it really eases the pain when someone seems to offer love—whether it is truly "love" or not. But the big problem is, we can't make people love us, especially when we need it the most and are the most unhappy.

In many marriages today, for example, a spouse who should be expressing love often doesn't and hurts the people closest to him or her. And the other spouse who should be there to provide love experiences such pain that he or feels unable to give love to the one who really needs it. Thus many people become terribly disappointed when the amount of love they wanted from their spouses in order to feel whole isn't given.

A TRUTH YOU CAN DEPEND ON

Because wrong thinking moves us into trying to cope with life's difficulties in the wrong ways, it makes sense that right thinking can get us out of a downward spiral. So I offer you a starting place, a truth that will keep you, protect you, and defend you when you are hurting.

Here it is: God loves you and me, has always loved you and me, will always love you and me, and will always take care of you and me. Do you believe that? If you do, acting on this truth will protect your heart and mind during times when you are hurting. You can depend on God rather than on something or someone else to help you escape difficulties. The truth is, no person or circumstance can provide what God can provide. He loves us and provides for us in ways that no one else can.

Even when we realize that God loves us just the way we are, though, it's so easy for us to concentrate on His punishment and judgment. This is especially true of deeply depressed people who feel worthless.

Not long ago a giant snowstorm swept into our area. I had my boots laid out and warming up as I prepared to conquer the snow and release my car from its frozen tomb.

My daughter Micaiah awoke, saw the snow, hurled herself into my boots, and ran outside without even putting on her coat or socks. A little while later, she came in dripping wet with my boots trailing behind her and the felt inserts awash in snow, slosh, and slush.

By this time I was ready leave. Not finding my boots, I called out, "Where are my boots?" Micaiah, as I soon learned, fled to her room. Then I found the boots, literally soaking in about three inches of "interior" water.

Angry, I went looking for Micaiah but saw my wife first. "Make sure she knows you love her anyway," Nancy reminded. (It's great to have a godly helper.) By the time I found Micaiah, she was sitting in her room, a panicked look on her face, awaiting the worst. I walked up to her, looked her in the face, and said, "Micaiah, I love you anyway."

She just looked at me and beamed. I, in turn, experienced one of those rare opportunities to affirm her when she was not prepared to be surprised by love. She had been thinking about judgment and punishment, but I was thinking about love—with a little reminder from Nancy.

This simple illustration reveals a profound truth. Just as Micaiah needed to be reminded of my love, we need to remember God's continuing love and care. We don't need to be reminded about punishment and judgment because we're already predisposed to think about them. We need to remember that God will continue to love us despite the fact that we may be thinking, *No one could love me.*

When we respond to God's love, He will see us through even during our darkest moments. He will empower us to take charge of our lives and become responsible for the choices we make. He will enable us to experience life fully and face our difficulties with joy. He will give us the courage to make godly decisions instead of allowing people and circumstances to unduly influence us.

PAUSE FOR REFLECTION

1. Consider this quote: "If we believe that our enjoyment of life is based on what people do to us, we are implying that they, not we, are responsible for the degree to which we experience quality of life." Do you agree or disagree? Why?

---

2. If you are allowing other people to affect your enjoyment of life, what are you willing to do to change that?

---

3. Reread Ephesians 3:17-19. What do these verses say about God and your relationship with Him?

---

4. Do you believe that God loves you and cares about your needs? If not, why not? If so, how is that influencing the way you live?

_____

_____

_____

What changes do you need to make in the way you face your needs?

_____

_____

5. Why do you think it's so important for Christians to obey God in all situations?

_____

_____

_____

In which situations should you respond differently, starting today?

_____

_____

6. Why do people find it easy to respond like powerless victims instead of allowing God to transform their lives?

_____

_____

_____

If you are doing this, how might you begin to respond differently?

_____

_____

7. What do you think or feel when you read Philippians 4:4?

_____

_____

_____

8. At some time in your life, did you become dependent on someone or something other than God in order to try to feel better and make life seem better? If so, describe that time:

_____

_____

_____

9. Are you committed to being dependent on God and putting "crutches" aside? Why or why not?

_____

_____

_____

If so, what changes would you like to start making today?

_____

_____

_____

12

Unleash the Bible's Transforming Power Through Song

The Bible has great power to transform your life. Singing the Psalms and/or reading them aloud reminds you of God's love and care for you. It is a great way to incorporate God's power and life-transforming truth into your life.

When you see an image and also hear a tune that accompanies the image, have you noticed that you usually remember both of them much longer than if you just hear or see each of them separately? Obviously television commercials use this technique, and marketers often broadcast brief segments from television commercials on the radio to reinforce advertising messages. Marketers know the potential impact of seeing and hearing something simultaneously.

We have the ability to remember images and sounds for long periods of time and can exercise control over what we choose to remember. Think about the music you enjoy. If a song is played that brings back memories of an event or person you enjoyed many years ago, that song almost immediately elicits positive emotions connected with that period of time. Just by listening to a certain song, you can remember many things from the past.

Some researchers believe that we record experiences in our minds in much the same way that records were organized in an old-time jukebox. The work of Penfield at McGill University strongly corroborates this conclusion.

To treat temporal lobe epilepsy, Penfield selectively froze small parts of patients' brains. In the process he discovered that as certain areas of the brains were stimulated, distinct memories—even those from the earliest times of life—were recreated in the patients' minds. These memories had not been collected in a large pool of memories but were neatly compartmentalized in specific areas of the brain.

This factor can help us take charge of our lives today. Just as we can change the radio stations, cassettes, or compact disks we're listening to, we can change our inner states from something painful and miserable to something much better just by changing what we listen to in life.

Let's say that you loved a person who recently died in a car accident. You can focus on his or her painful, tragic death. Or you can focus on what a great person he or she was and the wonderful times you spent together. One focus will inevitably create additional pain; the other focus will inevitably create joy in the midst of grief.

As I was seated in a home after a loved one died, family members and friends were experiencing terrible sadness until suddenly someone remembered something funny that the deceased person had done. Soon everyone howled with laughter. Were we being disrespectful or irreverent? Or were we choosing to experience joy and laughter in our loss?

Instead of immersing ourselves in the tragedies and pain of life, we can choose to rejoice in the Lord (Philippians 3:1) and to rely on His Word. We can change our negative perspectives. We can obtain a clue in how to do this from God, who told Cain to "do what is right" and receive His acceptance (Genesis 4:7). The Psalms give us a great place to start doing what is right, to start drawing close to God and applying His Word to our lives.

PLAYING THE SONGS OF GOD'S WORD INTO YOUR LIFE

The Word of God can be compared to a collection of powerful God-breathed songs that you can play anytime during your life. These songs in the Word of God can be played as records into your heart, giving you an entirely new repertoire of songs to focus on during times of difficulty. God's songs will touch your mind and your heart and transform your life.

The Word of God will lift you to a new place. It will set your foot "on a rock and give you a firm place to stand." (See Psalm 40:2.) When we despair, feeling as if we are falling into a miry pit and water is rushing over us, we can call out to God. He will place us on a solid rock and give us a firm place on which to stand. He will give us a way in which we can travel, a way established especially for us.

In a way the book of Psalms could be considered a gift of 150 life-giving compact disks from God to you that are meant for you to play day by day in accordance with the full glory of the saving mercy and joy that you have in Jesus Christ. When you play them, these songs will change your heart and mind, bringing positive changes into your life. But you have to reach out and play them instead of grasping for temporary things that may bring momentary pleasure but will in the long run bring pain.

When you learn how to "play" the Psalms, you can quickly, dramatically, and effectively control and discipline what you think and feel. The Psalms can remind you that even during your darkest moments, God will see you through and enable you to take charge of your life. You can use the Psalms when you feel discouraged or simply want to focus on God, who deeply loves you and is with you no matter what circumstance you face.

I know this because I've been reading and singing psalms for more than twenty years.

USING PSALM 20 AS AN EXAMPLE

Nearly every psalm contains helpful encouragement for troubled or despairing believers. Consider Psalm 20, for example, which addresses depression.

David wrote in the first verse, "May the Lord answer you when you are in distress." Another way to word this is, "May the Lord answer you when you are in *tsuris*." The Hebrew word *tsuris* conveys the meaning of "anguish," "affliction," or "deep depression."

He then continued, "May the name of the God of Jacob protect you." What does "the name of the God of Jacob" mean? This phrase should immediately remind us of Exodus 3 when God revealed Himself to Moses from within the burning bush. After telling Moses to take off his sandals, God stated, "I am the God of your father, the God of Abraham, the God of Isaac and the God of Jacob" (Exodus 3:6). Then He said that He had come down to rescue the Israelites from Egyptian bondage and had chosen Moses to be their leader.

Moses felt insecure and inadequate. In fact, he was afraid. "Who am I," he asked, "that I should go to Pharaoh and bring the Israelites out of Egypt?" (Exodus 3:11).

God replied, "I will be with you."

But Moses anticipated that he would face difficult challenges. "Suppose," he replied, "I go to the Israelites and say to them, 'the God of your fathers has sent me to you,' and they ask me, 'What is his name?' Then what shall I tell them?"

Patiently, God answered, "I AM WHO I AM. . . . Say to the Israelites, 'The Lord, the God of your fathers—the God of Abraham, the God of Isaac and the God of Jacob—has sent me to you.' This is my name forever" (Exodus 3:14-15).

The name for God that David used in Psalm 20 means the Eternal One. The psalmist expressed to us, in effect, "The Eternal God who delivered Israel miraculously, mightily, and powerfully from unbearable, unendurable slavery will hear you, answer you, be with you, and protect you." What a wondrous truth!

Many people become depressed because they have done kind, good things for people and have received no recognition for their actions. It's as if no one has seen what they have done. A friend of mine who is a police officer described to me how he risked his life to save another person's life. But no one thanked him—not the person, not the family, not even the police department. Yet about this same time, a politician saved a dog's life and received a write-up on the front page of the newspaper!

You may be facing great distress. Your friends or family members may have deserted you. All the people around you may have failed you. But you can always know that the Lord will attend to you. He will hear you, answer you, and protect you!

Next David wrote, "May he [God] send you help from the sanctuary and grant you support from Zion" (Psalm 20:2). Truly, when we're in trouble, we can expect the holy, merciful help of God to bless and protect us. He will send us help from the most sacred, holy place—from His heart.

Isn't that exciting! This life-giving truth gives us the infusion of hope we need in the midst of great trouble and distress. It conveys the picture of a person being rushed into an emergency room bleeding from a terrible injury. Suddenly he or she receives a blood transfusion and receives the gift of life.

When David wrote that God will grant us support from Zion, he reminded us that God sees everything that you and I do. The literal sense of this phrase is that He *records* all that we do. He sees and remembers all our sacrifices that seem to have affected no one and are noticed by no one. Our sacrifices haven't made the front pages of our local newspapers, but God has recorded them on the front pages of *The New Jerusalem Times*.

Next David reminded us of where our real joy comes from. It doesn't come from people's affirmations. It comes from God. Consider Psalm 20:5: "We will sing for joy over your victory, and in the name of our God we will set up our banners" (NASB). Paul expressed this same truth in Philippians 3:1 and 4:4: "Finally, my brothers, rejoice in the Lord! . . . Rejoice in the Lord always. I will say it again: Rejoice!"

Do you see this truth? Do you see how relevant this psalm is to your life? The focus of your joy is to be the Lord, not yourself, not your emotional state, not even your experience of happiness, satisfaction, or well-being at any given time. You and I are to rejoice in the Lord, in our salvation, because that is the basis of our joy. In spite of ourselves—our sinful thoughts, our confused feelings, our tough experiences—we possess a salvation in which we can rejoice.

What happens if we rejoice in how we *feel* at a given moment?

Chances are, we'll feel great now and horrible in a few days. Satan uses that "up and down" roller coaster to condemn, judge, and destroy us. Just think of the joy we can have regardless of how we feel at a given moment because of what God has done for us.

The joy David described is unrelated to circumstances. Let's say that you are in despair. Life doesn't seem worth living. But then you remember that you really do have something worth rejoicing over— you can rejoice in God and in His salvation. Suddenly, as verse 5 reveals, you are raising banners in the name of God. And as you do, you will become even more sharply focused on God as you turn to prayer. You will be moved to raise that banner in the name of God to pray. As you sing verses from the Psalms, you will be reminded that God will hear your voice and consider all your requests. What could be more encouraging than being a believer and knowing that God wants to continually bless you, to help you rise out of a despairing situation and be empowered?

Where will that power come from? David answered that, too: "Now I know that the Lord saves his anointed; he [God] answers him from his holy heaven with the saving power of his right hand" (Psalm 20:6). God responds from heaven with real saving power. He doesn't just "get you through" today, or even through your life. Rather, His purpose for you involves your full and perfect salvation, regardless of what you face and experience in this life. He literally answers "from his holy heaven with the saving power of his right hand."

It's important to realize that this is not just the power of positive thinking at work in your life. This is the power of God's Word and God's Spirit as He breaks into your life. It's rooted in a positive, personal, power-filled God who truly interacts with us. God, through His Word, prepares us to face anything in our lives with joy.

When He breaks into your life, I trust that you'll have powerful and positive responses to Him. When God does His saving work in your life, receive it as something positive. You have many positive things for which to be thankful (even though it can be hard to admit that sometimes), and God's salvation is the most positive of them all! As you recognize and take hold of God's great salvation and power, He will renew your mind so that you "will be able to test and approve what God's will is—his good, pleasing and perfect will" (Romans 12:2).

Sometimes in my seminars I ask, "Do you want to be depressed? How many of you want to be depressed?" And nobody raises a hand. Yet many people make choices that lead to depression. They play compact disks and cassettes packed full of melancholy lyrics. They watch movies filled with violence and sexual degradation. They focus their minds on bad memories, bad experiences, and seeming failures. They play the old songs of life that are filled with degradation, depravity, and corruption. But these old sinful songs are the songs of despair and defeat. Compare them to the "songs" God gives us through His Word.

FOCUS ON GOD AND HIS WORD, NOT YOURSELF

I began my career doing psychoanalytic psychotherapy. I was trained to help people free-associate, to say anything that came into their minds. I then had to interpret these associations in connection with the counselees' psychosexual stage of development, their relationships with their parents and significant other people, and most especially their relationship with me—their therapist. This interpretive process often went on for years, several times a week at great expense (for those who lasted that long).

Although most therapies are not as extensive or intensive as psychoanalytical treatment, they *are* committed to some extended probing into the counselee's deep-buried past. The assumption is that the counselee can't really be helped until he or she has relived past traumas, pains, and hurts. Based on the assumption that one's past experiences can build up to an explosive level if they are not reduced in some way, these therapies endeavor to facilitate a reliving and relieving of the pain. They aim to open up repressed negative memories, hoping that such reliving—and some measure of interpretation—will relieve the pain in each counselee's life. Often these therapies cannot acknowledge that one kind of behavior is better than another kind of behavior, so there is no direction—no absolute standards—toward which to guide counselees.

But does common sense reveal that we are at our best in life when we meet someone who asks us to describe the most terrible times of our lives? Does this interaction help us to live, behave, and perform better? My experience says no, and so does yours if you really think about it. Standard psychotherapies often produce more pain than they alleviate. People recycle themselves from therapist to therapist, from cure to cure, from one hopeful approach to the next hopeful drug.

The character portrayed by Woody Allen in one of his early movies, *Sleeper*, reflected on the 200 years his body had been frozen. He said, "If only I'd been in psychoanalysis all this time, I'd almost be cured by now."

Yes, the process of becoming more like Christ is a complex, life-consuming process that demands honest appraisal of thoughts and behaviors that have bogged you down in sin and misery. But the more time you dwell on what is bad, ugly, and hurtful and try to untangle the strands of your sin-filled life, the worse you will feel. That's why the apostle Paul commanded people to focus on the right things (Philippians 4:8-9).

If being absorbed in the miseries of life won't benefit us much, then what are we to do? The easiest thing is to forget about past miseries, to forget what is behind and strain toward what is ahead (Philippians 3:13).

Our lives are made up of various kinds of experiences. Some are good; some are bad. How you and I experience life today is determined to a great extent by how we respond to these experiences, not just what these experiences are. And the Bible gives us the tools we need not only to cope with our difficulties but even to thrive! It is God's Word—God-breathed, relevant truths from our Creator direct to us. As we've seen in a few verses of Psalm 20, Scripture is totally relevant to our lives. We need to focus on what it says, apply it to our lives through the Holy Spirit's indwelling power, and recognize how great our salvation really is.

It's easy for some people to overlook what God does for them, to boast in their own strength and power when they come out of the darkness of despair. But once you and I have discovered how easy it is to become lost in darkness and have emerged from that darkness through the power of God, we won't boast in our strength or power. We won't say, "Wow! Am I together! I can't believe how emotionally stable I am."

"Some trust in chariots and some in horses," David continued, "but we trust in the name of the Lord our God" (Psalm 20:7). Notice how personal these words are. We are to trust in the name of the Lord *our* God. We are not to boast in the chariots of our age—cars, wealth, positive thinking, Prozac, beautiful men or women, and so on. We are not to boast in anything earthly on which people rely. Our lasting defense against the despair of the world is never one of the things of the world. Beautiful cars rust. Beautiful men and women grow old. Beautiful money becomes worthless with inflation. Our lasting defense is our God—the eternal, ever-loving God Most High.

In verses 7-8 David revealed that people who "trust in chariots and . . . in horses" will be "brought to their knees and fall, but we rise up and stand firm." David understood that none of us can be raised upright and be despairing at the same time.

In a "Peanuts" cartoon, Charlie Brown was standing hunched over, saying, "This is my depressed stance." Then he said, "When you're depressed, it makes a lot of difference how you stand." Finally, he concluded, "If you're going to get any joy out of being depressed, you've got to stand like this."

In the psychiatric hospital in which I worked, a patient named Marvin consistently lay in a fetal position. I'd urge him to speak with me, but he wouldn't respond. Finally, I shouted, "Marvin, in the name of Jesus Christ, stand up!"

And you know what he did? He jumped up immediately and was no longer depressed. Why? Because he was enraged. "How dare you speak to me about Jesus?" he shouted. "I'm a Jew!"

Standing up positively changed Marvin's inner state, and it was the beginning of an external change, too. He came to understand Psalm 19:7: "Jehovah's perfect law restores the soul again."[1]

DON'T LET EXCUSES KEEP YOU
FROM PLAYING GOD'S SONGS

Sometimes people say something like this to me: "When I'm depressed, I don't want to read the Psalms. I don't have the energy. I don't care to open my Bible. The last thing I want to do is start singing the Psalms or even read them aloud."

"Okay," I may respond, "but why do you want to go deeper into depression? Why aren't you willing to do whatever it takes to get out of depression? You say you don't want to go into depression, but you don't take me seriously when I tell you to do what will move you out of it. What makes you think that you can't get out of it? The Psalms were written to help you get through your difficulties. Just getting up to get your Bible will start to make a change in your life. Opening it will make another change. Opening it to Psalm 20 will make another change. Opening to Psalm 37 will make another change. And doing things consistent with what the Psalms are saying, through the power of the Holy Spirit, will make all the change in the world."

Let's say that you are anxious, depressed, and angry and are looking for help. You could run to a counselor or psychologist. You could also run to Psalm 37, which reads, "Be still before the Lord and wait patiently for him; do not fret when men succeed in their ways, when they carry out their wicked schemes. Refrain from anger and turn away from wrath; do not fret—it leads only to evil" (vv. 7-8). David understood the connection between depression, worry, and anger and gave us incredible insight into our emotional states.

The Word of God can change a person's life faster than any antidepressant. God has given us the "songs" we need, but we need to listen to them—even when we don't "feel like it."

I wish that I could share with you face to face, eye to eye, and motivate you to pull out the book of Psalms and find the "right cassette" or "compact disk" that God has for you. As Moses put it, "I have set before you life and death, blessings and curses. Now choose life, so that you and your children may live" (Deuteronomy 30:19).

Will you choose death? Will you choose to remain depressed,

angry, anxious, afraid, confused, or . . . ? Will you luxuriate in self-pity and all that goes with it? Will you keep playing the old songs you used to listen to? Or will you consistently open your Bible to Psalm 20, Psalm 19, Psalm 37, or other psalms and apply what God has revealed?

Maybe you truly cannot sing the Psalms. If so, you can at least read them aloud. Doing that will make a tremendous difference in your life—and in the lives of others around you. Will you turn off the old songs and put on new ones? Remember, the apostle Peter wrote, "His [God's] divine power has given us everything we need for life and godliness" (2 Peter 1:3). Do you believe that?

Go and use what God has for you! "*Make every effort* to add to your faith goodness; and to goodness, knowledge; and to knowledge, self-control; and to self-control, perseverance; and to perseverance, godliness; and to godliness, brotherly kindness; and to brotherly kindness, love" (2 Peter 1:5-7, italics added). Choose to get out from under feelings and thoughts that wound and crush you. Make every effort to use and appreciate the gifts that God has given you. As a Christian, you are a son or daughter of light. Live in that light!

PAUSE FOR REFLECTION

1. What kinds of "songs" have you been listening to recently?

_____

_____

_____

2. Do you find it easier to rejoice in the Lord or to immerse yourself in the pain of your life? Why?

_____

_____

_____

_____

3. Have you ever sung some psalms or at least read them aloud? If so, what happened? If not, are you willing to try it?

_____

_____

_____

4. What does God promise to do when we call out to Him for help?

_____

_____

_____

5. What excuses do you use for not reading the Bible and praying?

_____

_____

_____

6. In what way do you rejoice in the salvation you have received through Christ?

_____

_____

_____

PART THREE

꙳

Take Control of Your Mind—
Your Thoughts
and Spoken Words

13

Tap into the Power of Accurate Biblical Thinking

A spiritual battle is taking place over your mind. Your thoughts—the words in your mind—have incredible power to disable or empower you. But you can choose how to think.

When Paul wrote, "Those who belong to Christ Jesus have crucified the sinful nature with its passions and desires" (Galatians 5:24), he revealed that we *already* can successfully exercise self-control and take charge of our lives!

It's a well-known fact that there is tremendous power in thinking. The Bible tells us that as a man thinks in his heart, so is he (Proverbs 23:7). Consider that statement! When you think something, that's what you are. You and I have the amazing power to determine what we are, but that power depends upon what we think. We can choose to think accurately or inaccurately.

What do you think would happen to an Olympic athlete who gets into the swimming pool to compete and thinks, *Gosh, I don't think I can swim my best time today*?

Think about a time when you heard someone say something about you that you didn't like and you allowed yourself to become unsettled about it until you were affected in negative ways. Or think about a time when you compared yourself to another person, thought you came up short, and gave up trying to improve. Or the time when you tried something new, failed at it, and said to yourself, *I'll never be able to do that anyway. There's no point in trying anymore.*

We've all thought negative thoughts about ourselves and other people. Some people literally spend years thinking negative thoughts about themselves, other people, and life. But you know what? We don't have to think negative thoughts. You and I can choose what kind of thoughts we will have!

I'm not just talking about positive thinking. I'm talking about the power of accurate biblical thinking, an activity strongly emphasized throughout the Bible. Paul clearly understood the value of positive thinking when he wrote, "Whatever is true, whatever is noble, whatever is right, whatever is pure, whatever is lovely, whatever is admirable—if anything is excellent or praiseworthy—think about such things" (Philippians 4:8).

Notice that this verse doesn't say, "Whatever is false, whatever is ignoble, whatever is wrong, whatever is impure, whatever is ugly, whatever is not to be admired—if anything is imperfect or not worth paying attention to—think about such things."

When you are around people who have a very positive outlook on life, what happens? How do you feel? They influence you in a positive way. Their joy is infectious. You enjoy being with them. In contrast, people who have negative thoughts about everything and are miserable all the time also influence you. Our culture has coined a term for these people. They're "downers." They are depressing to be around. Remember the expression: "Misery loves company"? I propose that this is not quite right. It should be: "Misery loves miserable company." A miserable person wants company that is as deeply despairing as he or she is.

Accurate biblical thinking invariably leads to biblical action, and biblical action is positive—even when it's hard to accomplish. For example, a woman came to me for help in dealing with an adulterous relationship. We talked together, and I asked her, "How do you feel about ending this relationship?"

"I feel terrible!" she exclaimed. "I know it's wrong, and I feel miserable, but part of me still wants to be with him."

Later after she broke off the sinful relationship, I asked her, "Are you glad that you broke it off?"

"Oh yes," she replied. "I was miserable. And the process was terribly hard. But I'm so glad I ended it."

You see, accurate biblical thinking contains positive thinking, but that isn't the end result. Paul understood this. Notice that he added these words after listing the positive things on which we are to think: "Whatever you have learned or received or heard from me, or seen in me—*put it into practice*. And the God of peace will be with you" (Philippians 4:9, italics added).

God calls us to put the good, positive things we are to think about into action! This is more than just the power of positive thinking. It is allowing the God of peace to empower us to live out biblical principles and take charge of our lives.

RECOGNIZE THE POWER OF DISABLERS

Unfortunately, many of us turn away from accurate biblical thinking and choose to disable ourselves by allowing debilitating thoughts to take up residence in our minds.

It seems silly for us to disable ourselves. But many of us in all walks of life and socioeconomic levels do it every day.

• Teenagers use crack.

• Parents reel in drunkenness.

• Marriage partners who began with a commitment to remain together for life turn against each other and commit adultery.

• Kids drop out of high school.

• Beautiful, "successful" people who seem to have "everything" commit suicide and overdose on drugs.

So many of us allow what I call "disablers" to enter our lives every day. These disablers are our debilitating thoughts. They zero in and destroy our days—and sometimes our lives and the lives of other people. They can make the difference between life and death, between placing well in the spiritual race of life and not placing at all. They can put us into mental hospitals and even destroy us.

We see disablers at work in a disgruntled employee who complains, "Here I am, spending my life in this rotten job," instead of taking steps to change jobs or at least appreciating the fact that he has a job. We see disablers at work in a husband or wife who asks, "Is my marriage really worth saving? What's the use anyway?"

I read a book not too long ago written by a prominent coach in which he described his work with champion athletes. He shared how the playing ability of the top ten internationally ranked tennis stars is absolutely indistinguishable. What makes the winning difference between them, he discovered, is not how they actually play on the court—their serves, volleys, speed, footwork, and so on. He figured out that the time they actually spend playing tennis is approximately 10 percent of the time they spend on the courts. What makes the difference between these ten players is not what they *do* during the actual playing time but what they *think about* on the court between volleys.

He is now able to predict with pretty good accuracy which players will lose their matches and which players will win by how they walk back to the line. Some of them walk with their shoulders stooped and heads down, muttering to themselves. He can visibly see the results of the thoughts that say, *This is no good. Things are going against me. I'm having a lousy day. I'll never win this set.*

This principle is at work in our lives, too. Have you noticed how much better you feel and often how much better situations become when you think positive thoughts instead of disabling ones? I have certainly seen how my positive or negative thoughts influence outcomes in my life.

For example, even though I'm not a fast runner, I have run a marathon and other races. Sometimes during those races I wrestle with disabling thoughts. Instead of fighting my way to the finish line, I have to admit that I sometimes think, *Why am I doing this? Why am I killing myself? I should be doing something else, shouldn't I?* Clearly such disabling thoughts don't help me win those races. But I can't blame anyone else for those thoughts. Saying I had that thought because everyone else was in front of me isn't a valid excuse either. I still could choose to think, *I only have so many people to pass before I'm at the front*, and then do everything I could to run a better race.

Some of you may remember a Canadian Olympic diver who froze on the high board in 1988. Standing up there, she was unable to even move—until a diver from the United States climbed up and spoke with her. Only then was she able to dive.

What stopped her from diving in the first place? We know the answer. It was a debilitating thought. Maybe she remembered that she had missed that dive during a practice three weeks earlier. Maybe she was thinking that she might make a fool of herself in front of five hundred million television viewers. Maybe, as she mentally prepared to do her complex routine, she kept thinking about one particular twist that she missed two days earlier. Maybe she worried about creating too much of a splash when she entered the water.

What her thought really was doesn't matter. What matters is that a disabling thought—not her ability nor an Olympic official—stopped her, and that another thought spoken to her got her moving again.

Maybe some of you are thinking that thoughts aren't really that important or powerful. Think about it! That Olympic diver had done that particular routine over and over, maybe thousands of times. She wasn't just a six-year-old kid approaching a diving board. She was an expert who had made many attempts. Her failure wasn't due to lack of talent and skill; it was due to a disabling, debilitating thought.

Only one thing makes her situation unique—it happened on international television. It happens all the time in our daily lives, but we often don't realize it. There is truly a spiritual battle for our minds.

THE BATTLE FOR OUR MINDS

For nearly thirty years, my work has centered on people and their problems. I have discovered that wherever I go, really desperate people approach me. Their distress is usually caused by inaccurate thinking.

Warren and Jane (names changed) came to me for counseling after she discovered that he had been having an extramarital affair. Warren indicated that he wanted to save his marriage, so he broke off the affair. After several sessions, Jane mentioned to me that she felt that his affections had been restored and were even renewed.

Then Warren telephoned me. "Although I'm doing what's right," he stated, "I'm still miserable. I can't control my thoughts about the other woman." Although his actions had changed, his thinking hadn't. He had decided to break off his immoral behavior but hadn't addressed the root of his thinking. His thoughts continued to focus on someone besides his wife, yet he wondered why he was desperate.

Mark, a man in his twenties, came to me for a completely different reason. He desperately wanted to get off drugs, but before long it became clear to both of us that the counseling wasn't working. Before he stopped coming for counseling, he told me, "As much as I want to stop, I'm also desperately trying not to stop."

Like many of us, Warren and Mark illustrate how thoughts keep us from becoming the men and women God calls us to be. Warren's thoughts and behavior were in conflict. Mark's thinking was contradictory. The greatest theologian of the Christian faith experienced and wrote about this same contradictory problem: "What I do is not the good I want to do; no, the evil I do not want to do—this I keep on doing" (Romans 7:19). A few verses later he wrote, "I see another law at work in the members of my body, waging war against the law of my mind and making me a prisoner of the law of sin at work within my members" (Romans 7:23).

I'm convinced that Paul did not write these words to hurl us into discouragement. Rather, he was describing the outer manifestation of the deep inner struggles—laws that waged war against his mind, imprisoning him. Notice the phrase "law . . . waging war against the law of my mind." Paul was left with a sense of being imprisoned. Both Warren and Mark and countless other people have talked with me about the same tensions.

James, the brother of Jesus, wrote that sin starts in a person's inner life, where he or she "is tempted when, by his own evil desire, he is dragged away and enticed. Then, after desire has conceived, it gives birth to sin; and sin, when it is full-grown, gives birth to death" (James 1:14-15). I believe he meant that a sinful action follows a sinful thought.

James focused on the sinful action, but what precedes such action gives it the opportunity to take root and grow. "Sin," James concluded, "gives birth to death." At that point, if there is no restoration, the matter becomes serious indeed. So we must put on the armor of God (Ephesians 6:10-17) and be alert (Ephesians 6:18).

It doesn't take a great deal of knowledge to realize that if we want to stop the pattern that leads to death, we'd better start in our minds. We need to stop destructive, ungodly thoughts at their very beginning.

Sinful thoughts compel and propel us in certain directions. If we allow them to take their course, we'll commit sinful acts. If we don't acknowledge debilitating, sinful thoughts for what they are and get rid of them, we allow ourselves to be deeply affected by them.

CHOOSING GODLY THOUGHTS

If we're honest with ourselves, we'll admit that negative, debilitating thoughts that lead to sin—and can even lead to physical and spiritual death—seem to hit us with the intensity and speed of enemy missiles. It's not as if we stand in our living rooms, see a disabling thought coming, and say to ourselves, *Okay, here comes a disabling thought. If I let it in, it's going to make me feel unhappy, so I'll sidestep it.*

In a sense, thoughts can be compared to emotions in that they both hit with power and can dominate our lives. Regardless of whether we believe we have generated our disabling thoughts or that they have come to us from other people, situations, satanic forces, and/or something we have seen or done, we still experience such thoughts.

Every day we are inundated by thoughts. They come at us from images and words that flash across the television screen, for example. They come at us from workplace conversations, song lyrics, billboards, books, and many other sources. Often these words and images revolve around consumerism, greed, lust, violence, quest for power, and immorality. Many people don't evaluate incoming thoughts. They think, *It's only a little image, a little scene, a little thought. I can handle it.* But they don't realize that over time the images and words they take in become the images and words that will replay over and over in their minds.

Have you ever watched a videotape and replayed a certain portion of it again and again? Instant replays are quite popular during sporting events, for example, because people want to see this angle or that angle. Likewise the images and words that enter our minds become the material we replay.

Trying to resolve the hurts, pains, injustices, and disappointments we have experienced, some of us replay them over and over in our minds. But in and of themselves, those negative experiences can never be completely made right in a way that can bring justice, fairness, rightness, and love. Why? Because these painful experiences have already happened. No matter how many times we work them through—what we wish that we or other people had done or said differently—the painful experiences themselves will never be any different.

RECOGNIZE THE POWER OF YOUR CHOICES

When I was about ten years old, I chose to watch science-fiction thrillers that played at the movie theater on Saturday afternoons. And without fail, I experienced weeks and even longer times of terror and nightmares after watching each one. I still remember a movie about outer space seed pods that took over a town. I also remember the main character in that movie and his name—Kevin McCarthy!

Why did I experience so much fear? Because of the choices I made. It's easy, though, to think that our thoughts have great power, almost as if we're just innocent bystanders watching our thought lives develop and erupt on their own.

Scientists send giant telescopes into outer space that can film the universe's outer reaches and send back pictures from thousands of light-years away. Researchers discover genetic secrets that enable us to heal diseases that were considered incurable just a few years ago. Yet few people (scientists included) seem able to exercise mastery over their thoughts.

I believe that the quality of the life you live is based on the quality of the choices you make—day by day, moment by moment. These choices include the thoughts that you think. If you choose to think about things that will bring grief, anxiety, fear, or despair into your life, what will your experience of life be like? Clearly it will begin to contain elements of grief, anxiety, fear, or despair.

How many Christian families today no longer choose to end each day with prayer and the reading of Scriptures and instead watch raunchy, disturbing television or video programs filled with images of blood and sex, fear and anger, loneliness and confusion? Would their lives improve if their minds were filled instead with truths from the Word of God? I don't think it takes much thought to answer this question.

You and I can choose whether or not we will view our thoughts as if they are actual entities in our minds, telling us to do things and showing us pictures. We can choose whether or not we will listen to our negative thoughts and allow them to disable us. We can choose the thoughts on which we will focus, and our thoughts will strongly influence our actions.

We see this ability to choose illustrated in the lives of Cain and Abel in Genesis 4. Abel, we recall, was a shepherd who brought portions of meat to sacrifice to God. Cain, a farmer, brought "fruits of the soil" instead. When God accepted Abel's offering but not Cain's, Cain became angry and downcast.

Remember what God said to Cain? "Why are you angry? Why is your face downcast? If you do what is right, will you not be accepted? But if you do not do what is right, sin is crouching at your door; it desires to have you, but you must master it" (Genesis 4:6-7).

Notice that God didn't wait for Cain to answer after asking those three questions. He didn't wait for Cain to say something like, "You didn't accept my sacrifice, God. You like my brother better than me." Rather, God got right to the heart of the issue, which our culture—and sometimes even the church—refuses to do. He said in effect, "Do what's right, and you'll be happy!"

But Cain soon killed his brother. His murderous actions didn't just materialize from thin air. They began with Cain's thoughts in which he saw himself as a victim. He considered himself to have received unfair treatment from God and became jealous of his brother. Cain's thoughts then led to sinful actions.

Real God-given power isn't what you exert over others. That's force. Real God-given power is what you exert over yourself. It's the ability to discipline yourself, to exercise control over not only your behavior but over your thoughts and emotions.

The fact that we can regain control of our thoughts should be really exciting to us. Taking control of our minds is nothing less than the ultimate discipline. And when we obey God—thinking and doing what's right according to His guidelines—we can be joyful no matter how difficult our circumstances may be.

Moses, the leader of the Israelites, understood how vitally important it is to choose godly thought patterns. He said to the people:

> Now what I am commanding you today is not too difficult for you or beyond your reach. It is not up in heaven, so that you have to ask, "Who will ascend into heaven to get it and proclaim it to us so we may obey it?" Nor is it beyond the sea. . . . No, the word is very near you; it is in your mouth and in your heart so you may obey it. See, I set before you today life and prosperity, death and destruction. For I command you today to love the Lord your God, to walk in his ways, and to keep his commandments, decrees and laws. . . . This day I call heaven and earth as witnesses against you that I have set before you life and death, blessings and curses. Now choose life, so that you and your children may live and that you may love the Lord your God, listen to his voice, and hold fast to him. For the Lord is your life, and he will give you many years in the land he swore to give to your fathers, Abraham, Isaac and Jacob. (Deuteronomy 30:11-16, 19-20)

There is no question that, in the ultimate sense, "to choose life" is to commit ourselves wholeheartedly to God. Yet I have counseled so many believers who heartily agree that they have "chosen life" and yet lack blessedness, joy, and peace. That is because they have failed to appreciate that choosing life has meaning for *today* as well as for *eternity*.

Right thinking brings the peace of God. Right thinking combined with right actions brings the God of peace. From Genesis through Revelation, the Word of God sends out the call of God to experience a life of joy, which results when you take charge of your sins, your fears, your doubts, and your failures. As you take charge of your mind, you'll see changes that you never thought nor dreamed were possible.

We often fail to appreciate that the decisions we make today concerning our thoughts will affect the quality of our lives in every way. Our thoughts don't have to control and dominate us unless we allow them to do so. The mental chaos that rules this world is not meant to rule the minds of Christians. God has given us the mind of Christ (1 Corinthians 2:16) and has given us His Spirit. Whereas "the mind of sinful man is death" (Romans 8:6), "the mind controlled by the Spirit is life and peace."

So let's see how we can, through the power of God, take control of our disabling thoughts and experience more abundant living. Let's follow Paul's example, who wrote that in all things he was taking charge of his life, exercising the control God had given him. You can win the spiritual battle for your mind and become the man or woman you are meant to be!

PAUSE FOR REFLECTION

1. What types of disabling thoughts have you allowed to remain in your mind?

_____

_____

_____

2. What impact have they had on your life? On the lives of other people?

_____

_____

_____

_____

_____

3. Describe a time when a positive thought turned a difficult experience into a better one.

_____

_____

_____

4. What choices are you making to put godly thoughts into your mind?

_____

_____

_____

5. What choices are you making that allow sinful thoughts to take root in your mind?

_____

_____

_____

14

Take Your Thoughts Captive

With God's help, you can gain control over your thoughts.
You must accept responsibility for confronting disabling
thoughts, take them captive, and choose to fill your mind
with godly images.

When disabling thoughts hit us hard, often we reel from the impact. Instead of acknowledging them for what they are and getting rid of them, however, we allow ourselves to be deeply affected by them. But is this just the "way life is"? Do we have to go through life unable to control our disabling thoughts?

No!

In the previous chapter, I wrote about how I watched scary science-fiction thrillers as a child and then had nightmares. Those experiences began teaching me a simple but important lesson. If I didn't see that kind of movie, I didn't experience terror at night. In a childlike way, I was learning what Solomon taught: "As he [a man] thinks within himself, so he is" (Proverbs 23:7 NASB).

So how can you and I triumph over our disabling thoughts?

PRINCIPLE 1:
ACCEPT RESPONSIBILITY FOR YOUR THOUGHTS.

You have the ability to exercise control over your thoughts. Even if you don't realize it, you have a kind of control button that allows you to take or relinquish control over your thoughts. God warned Cain to focus his mind on the right things. But Cain chose to think about the wrong things—anger, jealousy, and so on—which led to his murderous actions. Before you read any further, ask yourself this question: *Right now am I willing to admit that I can, with God's help, regain control of my thoughts and think enabling thoughts instead of disabling ones?*

Shortly after Paul urged Christians to rejoice in the Lord always, he explained that if a Christian prayerfully, earnestly, and thankfully presents his or her requests to God, then God's peace will guard that person's heart and mind (Philippians 4:6-7). That means that joy, the fruit of the Spirit, is a byproduct of how we think. Receiving joy is not just something that happens by accident. It's not just something we wake up with in the morning. Accepting responsibility for our thoughts is the first step in gaining control of them.

PRINCIPLE 2: TO EXPERIENCE LASTING CHANGE, YOUR MIND—NOT JUST YOUR BEHAVIOR—MUST CHANGE.

The Hebrew Scriptures use the word translated "heart" to describe the depth of a person's inner being—the core of who we are. In order for a person to experience meaningful, significant, and lasting change in life, his or her heart must change. So to change one's thoughts requires a change of heart—a radical transformation through the power of the Holy Spirit.

Jesus clearly linked a person's love for Him with obedience to His teachings and the Scriptures. "If you love me," He told the disciples, "you will obey what I command" (John 14:15). Yes, God calls you and me to change sinful behavior that does not honor and please Him. As important and good as behavioral change is, however, taking charge of one's mind and life involves much more.

Paul wrote that we are to discipline ourselves for the sake of godliness. Behavior is one aspect of godliness, but godliness also involves our minds—our thoughts—and hearts. So discipline that leads to godliness, I'm convinced, must include our thinking. We have to work on disciplining our minds from which our behaviors stem, rather than primarily focusing on outward behavior. We have to allow God to transform us by the renewing of our minds (Romans 12:2).

PRINCIPLE 3: DETERMINE TO THINK THROUGH
YOUR LIFE-DOMINATING PROBLEMS IN THE CORE OF YOUR
BEING RATHER THAN JUST REACTING TO THEM.

People who are "successful"—among the people of God and in society at large—seldom just stumble from success to success. Their biographies reveal that they fail time and time again. Yet, they say, each time they learn something new, something valuable, something they can use during the next opportunity. So examining our failures can contribute greatly to the joy we experience in life.

You have a choice today. When you experience difficult challenges, you can react to them and think yourself right into despair every time. You can say, "What a complete failure I am. I guess I'll never do anything right." Or you can look forward to the next opportunity and say, "Wow, did I learn from that failure!"

Where else does it lead if you say, "I'll never do anything right"? The odds are that train of thought will move to "I'm a failure as a person" and then to this: "I can do nothing to stop this. I have no power over being a failure. In fact, why bother trying? My life will be one big failure. I might as well accept that. Nothing will ever change."

Have you had similar thoughts? Does this train of thought seem familiar? Is this the way you sometimes react to situations? Are these the disabling thoughts you choose? You don't have to get trapped by disabling thoughts. You are capable of getting out of your shame, despair, hopelessness, anger, and so on. That can be accomplished by taking control of your thoughts.

Consider Susan, for example. A fine Christian woman, she came to me because she was deeply troubled by blasphemous, terrifying thoughts that caused her to experience extreme self-accusation, paralyzing fear, and despair. "I have these evil thoughts about God," Susan sobbed tearfully, "and so I can't be a Christian. I've been thinking that God is just waiting to hurl me into hell because of them." As she and I thought through her situation, it became clear that she had no area of known sin that would have led to these thoughts. Tired of reacting to them, she longed to be at peace, to have godly thoughts. So she took steps to learn where they came from. Instead of continuing to be victimized by them, she learned to confront them.

PRINCIPLE 4: TAKE YOUR DISABLING THOUGHTS CAPTIVE THROUGH CONFESSION AND THE EMPOWERMENT OF GOD.

I helped Susan understand that her thoughts were not sovereign, that they didn't need to dominate her life. Only God is sovereign! The apostle Paul taught us how to handle invading thoughts in 2 Corinthians 10:4-5: "The weapons we fight with are not the weapons of the world. On the contrary, they have divine power to demolish strongholds. We demolish arguments and every pretension that sets itself up against the knowledge of God, and we take captive every thought to make it obedient to Christ." We are to "overcome evil with good" (Romans 12:21).

It wasn't enough for Susan to confess her negative thoughts to God and try to think about godly things. She had to strive to live a life pleasing to God. She had to take her thoughts captive each time they popped into her mind. She had to live by faith, trusting that she could continue to live as a child of God in spite of her disabling thoughts. She had to remember that she had been saved by grace through faith in Jesus. She had to actively repudiate her disabling thoughts and change her interpretation of them. She had to remind herself of her love for God. By the Holy Spirit's power, she had to overpower and replace the evil thoughts flooding her mind with godly ones.

Yes, Susan had rotten thoughts about God. But realizing that fact is quite different from maintaining the belief that she was rotten. It is one thing to say, "Everything I believe about myself as a child of God must be a lie because I thought this." It's quite another thing to say, "I know that I love God, so these thoughts can't be trusted because they are alien to who I know myself to be as a person and to what I know about the character of God."

If you are beset by disabling thoughts, ask God to help you gain control over your thoughts, to guide you in the process of directing your thoughts in directions that will honor Him. In His power, you can take disabling thoughts captive!

PRINCIPLE 5: YOU NEED THE MIND OF CHRIST.

Paul wrote in Philippians about people's struggles with pride and self-concern. He used this expression in Philippians 2:5: "Let this mind be in you, which was also in Christ Jesus" (KJV).

It's interesting that the word translated "mind" means "thoughts" or "attitude." The antidote to the kind of thinking that leads to sin and death is to think like Jesus Christ. So in order to develop the kind of minds we need to have in dealing with the enormous problem of sin and the radical consequences sin has on our thinking, we need the mind of Christ.

Everything in your life revolves around what you focus your thoughts on! In Romans 8:5 Paul wrote, "Those who live according to the sinful nature have their minds set on what that nature desires; but those who live in accordance with the Spirit have their minds set on what the Spirit desires." Each day ask God to give you the mind of Christ, to help you think godly thoughts.

PRINCIPLE 6: CHOOSE TO FOCUS YOUR THOUGHTS
ON THE RIGHT THINGS.

I have studied a great amount of holocaust-related material. The Jews involved lost everything—their families, their fortunes, their lives. Yet Jewish survivors have testified time and time again that in the midst of the cesspool of evil in which they found themselves, they saw, heard, or experienced a thought, word, or image so ennobling that it spoke to their souls, turned them around, and produced within them a will to live. "Thoughts make a person free," one survivor said recently. "The Nazis couldn't take away our thoughts."

How true! We recall again these words of the apostle Paul: "Whatever is true, whatever is noble, whatever is right, whatever is pure, whatever is lovely, whatever is admirable—if anything is excellent or praiseworthy—think about such things" (Philippians 4:8). And when we do this, "the God of peace" will be with us (Philippians 4:9).

What a stark contrast there is between the words in this verse—

true, noble, right, pure, lovely, admirable, excellent, praiseworthy—and the words that capture the attention of millions of people today. Sad to say, many people today seem to be more transfixed—more consumed—by evil than by good and beauty. I have to assume that these people want to experience pain because they spend so much time and energy focusing on what is awful, ugly, depressing, and discouraging.

Will focusing on the wrong things accomplish any good in your life? Is such a focus biblical? Do the Scriptures urge you to be mired in misery? No! You have the power to focus on what is good and beautiful or on what is bleak and ugly. It's your choice.

As Christians, most of us want our lives to be characterized by what is true, good, and beautiful. The problem is, we may want a movie, television show, or how-to formula to accomplish this for us rather than committing ourselves to disciplining our minds. The real secret, which Paul learned, lies in our ability to live a Spirit-filled life. Only then can we be permanently joy-filled and Spirit-filled. Only then will we hunger to think the right thoughts and flee from thoughts that do not honor God.

Are you willing to take charge of your thoughts and develop thought patterns consistent with biblical models—those that are true, noble, right, pure, lovely, admirable, excellent, and praiseworthy?

It's not easy to retrain your thoughts. It's not easy to respond in new Christlike ways. It's not easy at first to direct your mind toward godly things. But take heart! As God empowers you to focus your mind on the right things, it will become easier.

You can develop a new frame of reference. A frame is only a boundary for what is placed within it. Your frame of reference should contain a portrait filled with all that is true, noble, right, pure, lovely, admirable, excellent, and praiseworthy. Since it is *your* frame of reference, you can decide what goes into the frame! Disabling thoughts might hit you like missiles, but they don't have to stay in your mind!

God is willing to empower you to take control of your thoughts. He loves you so much that He sent His Son to die for you and promises to be with you no matter what your situation may be. He wants you to be released from disabling thought patterns and be transformed by the renewing of your mind. He will actively renew our minds if we ask and allow Him to do it.

PAUSE FOR REFLECTION

1. What types of situations, relationships, music, videos, and so on trigger disabling thoughts within you?

_____

_____

_____

2. What do you think it means to accept responsibility for your thoughts?

_____

_____

_____

3. Do you really believe that if you prayerfully, earnestly, and thankfully present your requests to God, His peace will guard your heart and mind? What difference does this truth make in your life?

_____

_____

_____

4. Describe five things you learned recently from difficult situations.

_____

_____

_____

_____

_____

_____

5. Which negative thoughts do you need to confess to God?

_____

_____

_____

6. What are the benefits of having your mind focused on what the Holy Spirit desires instead of on what your sinful nature desires?

_____

_____

_____

7. When you read Philippians 4:8, how did those words compare to the thoughts you have in your mind?

_____

_____

_____

15

Triumphing over Anxiety

By living for God one day at a time, you can triumph over your anxiety.

In the lives of many people, anxiety is a great disabler. A pervasive problem, it affects people of all ages, socioeconomic groups, and nationalities. The word *anxiety* means "to rip," "to divide," "to tear apart." Anxiety causes people to feel as if they are being ripped to pieces.

Unchecked anxiety will cause you to lose control in the battle for your mind. It will make you sick, depressed, tired, joyless, and in many ways lifeless. You can't take charge of your life and focus in the right direction if anxiety is tearing you apart and robbing you of joy.

A recent book encouraged readers to get rid of their anxiety by getting rid of whatever makes them anxious—including their spouses! But is that the best solution? Can we really deal with anxiety by running away? By destroying relationships? By quitting our jobs?

Jesus has taught us a better way. Knowing how prone people are to worry, He taught His disciples how to face anxiety in Matthew 6. There we read about key causes of anxiety and how to deal with them.

CAUSE #1: A PREOCCUPATION WITH OUR PHYSICAL NEEDS

Many people today face difficult times. They don't have enough food and clothing, so they put all of their energy into worrying about how to obtain these basics.

Jesus understood that we need clothing and food but recognized that seeking after spiritual truth is more important. After stating that God can feed and clothe His people, Jesus said, "Who of you by worrying can add a single hour to his life? . . . So do not worry, saying, 'What shall we eat?' or 'What shall we drink?' or 'What shall we wear?'" (v. 27, 31). He challenged us, in other words, to look to Him for what we need rather than being preoccupied with obtaining earthly things that will not last. "I give food and shelter to the birds," He said, in effect, "and I splendidly clothe the lilies of the fields in beauty. What are they compared to you? Surely I'll take care of you. I know you and I love you" (Matthew 6:26, 28-29).

CAUSE #2: A LUST FOR EARTHLY THINGS WE DO NOT YET HAVE

Jesus continued in verse 32, "The pagans run after *all these things,* and your heavenly Father knows that you need them" (italics added). It's easy, even for Christians, to crave material things and to become anxious in the process. In these days of easy consumer credit, we all know what can happen to people who overextend themselves financially. We know what happens to a family when a spouse puts more emphasis on obtaining material things than he or she does on building relationships with family members. We've seen people who frantically work several jobs and never seem to get caught up on anything. Instead of pursuing "these things," we are called to pursue greater faith in Him.

CAUSE #3: A LACK OF FAITH

Verse 32 also reveals that we become anxious when we don't really believe in God's unchanging character. Even though our heavenly Father knows that we need basic essentials and wants to meet our needs, we find ourselves responding as if we must provide everything for ourselves. We find it easy to forget what Paul taught in Romans 8:31-32: "If God is for us, who can be against us? He who did not spare his own Son, but gave him up for us all—how will he not also, along with him, graciously give us all things?" It's as if we believe we're guilty if we don't fret, pace nervously, and wring our hands when we lack essentials.

We are called to display our great confidence in our great God—in the workplace, with our families, in service to other people. We are to become people who will walk around with the praise of God on our lips and in our hearts.

CAUSE #4: DWELLING ON FUTURE UNCERTAINTIES BEYOND OUR CONTROL

Another reason we experience anxiety is that we allow our minds to dwell on the future, over which we have little control. We can become plagued by common worries such as, "Will I have a job next year?" "What if my child becomes terminally ill?" "What if someone causes me to have an accident?" "What if I get arthritis and can't work?" "What if my spouse leaves me for someone else?"

Continuing to teach us how to deal with stressful circumstances, Jesus said, "Seek first his [God's] kingdom and his righteousness, and all these things will be given to you as well" (Matthew 6:33). Then He continued, "Therefore do not worry about tomorrow, for tomorrow will worry about itself. Each day has enough trouble of its own" (Matthew 6:34).

Jesus understood that life is comprised of more than food, clothing, and shelter. We are to live with the spiritual dimension of life foremost in our minds. We are not to focus on material things. After all, we are not "of this world."

Regardless of its source, anxiety results in physical and spiritual destruction. It will tear you up and consume you—your time, your attention, your thoughts, and your life. It will remove you from the present, in which you can exercise some control and experience joy, and move you into an uncertain future over which you have no control. Anxiety will direct you away from the unchanging character of God and toward your frailties.

TAKE CHARGE OF YOUR ANXIETY

So since no individuals in the world except Adam and Eve have known what it's like to have no anxiety, how can we be free from it? Remember, Jesus told His disciples four times in Matthew 6 to have no anxiety: "Do not worry about your life" (v. 25), "Who of you by worrying can add a single hour to his life?" (v. 27), "So do not worry, saying, . . ." (v. 31), and "Therefore do not worry about tomorrow . . ." (v. 34). He really wanted to get this point across. "Stop being anxious," He said in effect. "It won't help you, it's sinful, and it's robbing you of what life with Me is all about."

Since anxiety means "to be distracted," "divided," or "torn apart," it makes sense that having no anxiety means being single-focused, single-purposed. Once you have done everything you can do to accomplish what God has set before you, you don't have to be weighed down and burdened by a problem you cannot solve at a particular time. You can focus on God, in whose eyes you are much more significant than the birds and the lilies of the field.

You see, we don't have to become anxious about whether or not we can keep all the details of our lives running smoothly. We didn't start our lives, for example, and we must view everything that comes to us as His provision—even, and perhaps especially, during difficult and/or perilous times.

Nothing we can do, said Jesus, can add a single hour to our lives. Not the best thoughts. Not the best attitudes. Nothing. So we can face today with courage and confidence, with joy and freedom in the Lord. Instead of being anxiously consumed with earthly life, we are called to pursue what the Christian life is all about—the life of faith.

God calls us to recognize that life is to consist of much more than anxiously seeking "all these things." This doesn't mean that we can become careless with our lives, however. Rather, it means that we are not to live as if this life is all there is. God calls us to pursue a greater faith. This faith is not rooted in ourselves but in the character of God.

If you have faith in God, you will know that God knows you personally and that He loves you. Knowing this means that you will never remain anxious. Situations that used to create anxiety will also lose their hold over you.

Paul told us the secret of how to face whatever comes along without feeling anxious: "I have learned to be content whatever the circumstances. I know what it is like to be in need, and I know what it is to have plenty. I have learned the secret of being content in any and every situation, whether well fed or hungry, whether living in plenty or in want" (Philippians 4:11-12). What was his secret? "I can do everything through him [Christ]," he wrote, "who gives me strength" (Philippians 4:13).

What empowers us to triumph over anxiety is not our own strength and willpower. It is Christ Himself. He alone is our sufficiency.

THE ALTERNATIVE TO ANXIETY

The alternative to feeling anxious is so simple, yet profound. As Jesus said, we are to live one day at a time for God. Each day provides all the trouble it can handle.

Based on their beliefs, existentialists distorted this concept and said, "Okay, live for today and the moment because that's all there is. Nothing has meaning. The future and past have no meaning."

Remember Joan Baez, who sang, "I live one day at a time; I dream one dream at a time; yesterday is dead and tomorrow is blind, so I live one day at a time"?

Jesus described a completely different way to live—living for God. When we live one day at a time for God, we won't remain anxious about our earthly existence. Yes, the past is real and has consequences. The future is real, too, and hopefully you and I are leaving godly legacies for future generations. But we can be free to live each day with joy, knowing that God is with us.

Regardless of the past or the future, you can be sure that God has given you this moment! If you live for more than that, you are making a big mistake. Remember the parable in Luke 12 about the man who completely filled up his barns with crops and then made plans to build bigger barns? "And I'll say to myself," he said, "'You have plenty of good things laid up for many years. Take life easy; eat, drink and be merry.'"

What happened to this man, who decided to find security in the crops he could put into his barns? "You fool!" God said. "This very night your life will be demanded from you."

How can you be ready for God today if you are consumed with the cares of tomorrow? One of the greatest theologians, Jonathan Edwards, said, "I will endeavor to never do anything now, which I would never do were it the last hour of my life." This puts an entirely new perspective on things, doesn't it?

You and I are always in the mind of God. He knows our thoughts and actions. Thus in effect we are always standing before Him. So why don't we trust in His character and stop being anxious?

ANTIDOTES TO ANXIETY

Let's look at five easy ways to focus your mind on God and not on your anxieties:

• Focus on today. "This is the day the Lord has made; let us rejoice and be glad in it" (Psalm 118:24). Focus on the positive things that are happening in your life.

• Be thankful to God. "Do not be anxious about anything, but in everything, by prayer and petition, with thanksgiving, present your requests to God" (Philippians 4:6). Paul understood the nature of mankind. He knew that it's impossible for you to be anxious and thankful simultaneously.

• Keep a biblical focus. "Whatever is true, whatever is noble, whatever is right, whatever is pure, whatever is lovely, whatever is admirable—if anything is excellent or praiseworthy—think about such things" (Philippians 4:8).

• Take action. "Whatever you have learned or received or heard from me, or seen in me—put it into practice," Paul wrote (Philippians 4:9). You are not just supposed to think biblically. You are to act righteously—to do right. God calls you to act responsibly in dealing with areas of your life where anxiety surfaces.

• Maintain your focus on God. When you keep that focus, "the God of peace" will be with you (Philippians 4:9). You can take Him at His word and "cast all your anxieties on him because he cares for you" (1 Peter 5:7).

You have a choice today. Will you live the rest of the day thankfully? Will you focus your mind on the right things and act righteously? Will you keep God and His promises clearly in mind? Will you take anxieties and mentally lift them up to Jesus? He says that you can do it, and He's glad to carry them for you.

PAUSE FOR REFLECTION

1. Which situations tend to make you anxious?

_____

_____

_____

Take a few moments right now to talk with God about them.

2. What actions can you take, in God's power, to help reduce your anxiety level?

_____

_____

_____

3. List a few of the things that God has done for you that reveal His loving care for you.

_____

_____

_____

_____

4. What changes will you begin to make so that you can focus on the challenges of today instead of worrying about tomorrow?

_____

_____

_____

5. If you knew that Jesus will return within thirty days, which material things would you stop pursuing?

_____

_____

_____

6. In what ways do you demonstrate your living faith on a daily basis?

_____

_____

_____

7. Is the praise of God "always on your lips?" Why or why not?

_____

_____

_____

16

Harnessing the Power of Words

The words you think and speak are powerful. Start choosing today to stop using words in your thoughts and speech that harm you and/or other people. Replace such words with godly words that encourage and uplift.

Remember this taunt: "Sticks and stones can break my bones, but words can never hurt me"? The reason everyone remembers these words is that everyone knows they are a pack of lies! We know that some of the worst pain we've experienced has come because people aimed mean, cruel words at us.

On some level we all know the power of words. They may not kill, but they can crush a person's spirit and destroy him or her in other ways. The words we hear and say have a profound impact on the thoughts we think! So if we're going to take control of our thoughts, we also need to consider the power of words.

The right words can motivate a team or army to reach heights of performance they never thought they could achieve. Words can soothe a hurt, make someone laugh, and convey deep passion and love. Or words can completely discourage, defeat, or even disgrace someone— even yourself—and keep reminding you of your seeming failures, weaknesses, and shortcomings.

James recognized how difficult it can be for us to take charge of our words. "With the tongue we praise our Lord and Father," he wrote, "and with it we curse men, who have been made in God's likeness. Out of the same mouth come praise and cursing. My brothers, this should not be. Can both fresh water and salt water flow from the same spring? My brothers, can a fig tree bear olives, or a grapevine bear figs? Neither can a salt spring produce fresh water" (James 3:9-12).

Again we go back to the importance of our *perspective*. When NASA heard that the *Apollo 13* space team would probably die from carbon monoxide poisoning, one leader said, "This is going to be NASA's greatest defeat." The other said, "This is going to be NASA's finest hour." They were looking at the same situation but from different perspectives. The words of one man displayed his despair. The words of the other man displayed his confidence, a confidence that motivated the entire ground team to discover solutions to the space team's numerous problems.

Each of us can choose our perspective in every situation we face. The words we use will clearly demonstrate the choice we've made— whether we've chosen despair or hope, hatred or love, sadness or joy, fear or courage.

Of course, our words reflect more than our inner commitments and feelings. Our words also help to form the beliefs, commitments, and destinies of everyone who hears them. Our words, even if we're not great or famous people, have tremendous effects. Which of us isn't moved when we contemplate Christ hanging on the cross and saying, "Father, forgive them, for they do not know what they are doing" (Luke 23:34)? Or when we picture Stephen who, while being stoned to death by a mob, cried out as he lay dying, "Lord, do not hold this sin against them" (Acts 7:60)? Or when Martin Luther, who had been ordered to recant, declared boldly, "Here I stand"?

Our words are significant. That's why Paul wrote, "Do not let any unwholesome talk come out of your mouths, but only what is helpful for building others up according to their needs, that it may benefit those who listen" (Ephesians 4:29).

Paul understood firsthand the dangers of careless words. That's also why he wrote that we are to think about "whatever is true, whatever is noble, whatever is right, whatever is pure, whatever is lovely, whatever is admirable" and what is excellent and praiseworthy (Philippians 4:8). He knew that in order to think and speak only the right words, we needed to begin by saying those words to ourselves.

WHAT ARE YOU REALLY SAYING TO YOURSELF?

Have you noticed that if you sincerely tell someone something beautiful, those words most often lead to an experience that is uplifting and beautiful? Conversely, if you speak words in anger and contempt, you may create a bitter situation. The outcome often originates within you!

Just as our thoughts are expressed in our words, our words are expressed in our thoughts. Words help to form thoughts, which have certain actions attached to them. If you entertain happy thoughts, you will likely exhibit numerous actions connected with happiness. Perhaps you will smile, be peaceful, or be generous. If you entertain angry thoughts, on the other hand, you might gnash your teeth, speak loudly using harsh words, or clench your fists.

Take a few moments right now and write down what you are thinking and saying about yourself (and to others) that is false, evil, ugly, and will ultimately tear yourself down or hurt other people. What kind of a list did you come up with?

Now realize that you can exercise control over your mental and spoken thoughts! If you think and speak rotten words, it is because you have chosen to do so. Don't blame your wrong use of words on other people, on what they may have done to you. That's their responsibility. Instead, recognize that you are responsible for how you think and how you respond.

Why do you respond in one way or the other? On some level, you decide that a certain response is more beneficial or necessary than another one. Then you develop a pattern of belief that demonstrates what you want to come your way in certain situations by responding in certain ways.

YOU CAN CHANGE WHAT YOU THINK AND SAY

Habitually sinful ways of responding don't have to hold you captive. For example, you don't have to be habitually depressed, angry, or anxious. *But I feel like I can't help myself,* you may be thinking. *I've*

learned how to think and say things that hurt other people and myself.
They come out of my mind and my mouth before I can do anything
about them.

As difficult as it may seem, such habits can be changed! And you
can do that by becoming conscious of what you think and say. You can
begin to monitor yourself and change the language you may have used
all your life. Maybe a certain situation makes you want to explode, like
when a family member is late getting into the car for church, a loud
family pulls into the public campground at two in the morning and
wakes you up by yelling, or a driver cuts you off in traffic. Instead of
letting the anger surge, try thinking, *Boy, this isn't worth getting mad*
about. Which edifying words can I focus on that will help me be gra-
cious in this difficult situation?

Situations, remember, don't make you furious. A situation is just
that—a situation. You can choose how you will think and speak about
it and how you will respond to it. Does a challenging situation have to
ruin your day? Or can it challenge you to think about all the blessings
you have?

Negative thought and speech patterns can be changed. They don't
have to lead to sinful, negative words in your mind and speech. But each
of us has to stop making excuses for our sinful language and actions.

This truth was reinforced when I read the story of a fifty-year-old
man named Robert. A former boxer who spent years on the street as a
drunk, he began to change his life when he poured out his lunch—half
a gallon of vodka—on the ground. Soon afterward he began helping
other people. His thirteen-step program restores one in every three drug
abusers or drunks to society, and it only costs $3,000 per year to oper-
ate. Compare this to governmental detoxification programs that can cost
more than $15,000 per person and usually accomplish little or nothing.

The sign that greets anyone entering Robert's program is, "The day
you stop making excuses, that's the day you start a new life." This principle applies to an alcoholic—and to you and me. Have you ever wondered why people continue to think, say, and do things that inevitably
destroy them? They draw on a basketful of excuses that allow them to
perpetuate sinful thoughts and deeds that they don't want to change.

Not long ago I was featured on a live radio call-in show, and a caller asked why he continued to use crack even though he'd been through every treatment imaginable and really wanted to get off it.

"You don't really want to get off crack," I answered, "but you like the idea of wanting to get off crack. You like taking crack more than you like actually never using crack again."

Sad to say, he agreed. He was saddened because he had been telling himself that he wanted to get off crack, but it was frightening for him to realize just how much he loved the experience of getting high. I blew the cover off the words he used to deceive himself and others.

YOU CAN CHANGE WHAT YOU TELL YOURSELF

Once you commit yourself to stop using words in your mind and speech that allow you to continue thinking, saying, and doing things that harm you and/or other people, use this follow-up principle: Change what you tell yourself about your experience or situation.

For example, Robert remained a drunk as long he told himself things such as, *I can never win; by drinking I can avoid all the rat-race hassles; I won't mess up anyone else's life,* and so on. But finally he used the power of his words to ask, "What am I doing with my life?" Then he honestly answered his question by admitting that he was destroying it. By applying truth to his life, Robert was finally able to move away from giving the worst possible meaning to his experience. Today he continues to positively impact other people.

YOU CAN REDIRECT YOUR WORDS

Once you change what you tell yourself, you can redirect what you say. Redirecting your words involves using speech designed to redirect *you* onto a path that enables you to handle a difficult situation with more grace, self-control, and love, and less anger, bitterness, and/or despair. Redirection will help you deal with what actually happens in a situation rather than with how you feel about what happens. It will help to keep you from speaking to yourself words filled with pain, rage, and bitterness.

The path of grace and edification is far removed from the path of self-defeating, self-destructive words. It's time to leave the sinful, self-defeating, self-destructive path we've developed through our habitual ways of responding. It's time to redirect our words.

You and I do not have a responsibility to "be true to ourselves." Rather, we have a responsibility to be true to God—to die to self! That process of dying to self often involves putting to death many negative, destructive thoughts and words that come to our consciousness. It's a proven fact that if you redirect your words when you are twisted up by a swirl of violent emotion, they can become a language of edification—a language that meets the needs of the situation and actually provides grace to your listeners. We can create new experiences for ourselves if we let ourselves experience things in new ways, in ways that edify and provide grace according to the needs of the moment.

Recently I was in a foreign country to do a counseling seminar. The driver of the car I was riding in unintentionally blocked the view of a woman in another car who intended to make a turn. Even though we spoke a different language, it was clear as we looked at each other that she was thinking, *I hate you,* and was cursing a mile a minute. The veins on her neck bulged out; she glared with hatred as the unheard words tumbled out of her mouth. What happened next? The driver of my car looked at her and smiled, and then she smiled, too.

This illustrates what it means to redirect our words. What really happened is simple to understand. The woman was disarmed by my driver's smile and could not help but return it. Earlier she had probably imitated drivers who had been rude and nasty to her. But now she was becoming courteous to him even though at first she had responded rudely. Possibly this new pattern of response manifested itself in the next difficult situation she faced while driving—and maybe it even spread to situations when she wasn't driving—such as at work or in her home. But notice, on the most basic level, that an imitation took place!

As Christians, we are supposed to imitate Christ. "Be imitators of God, therefore, as dearly loved children and live a life of love, just as

Christ loved us and gave himself up for us as a fragrant offering and sacrifice to God" (Ephesians 5:1-2). When we imitate Christ, we can defuse more conflicts than we might imagine.

What words did Christ use that are to be the models for us to imitate?

• *"Blessed* are the merciful, for they will be shown mercy" (Matthew 5:7, italics added).

• *"Follow me"* (Luke 5:27, italics added).

• "I tell you the *truth"* (Matthew 8:10, italics added).

• "I am the way and the truth and the *life"* (John 14:6, italics added).

• "Seek first his *kingdom* and his *righteousness"* (Matthew 6:33, italics added).

When you compare the Lord's vocabulary to your own, where are your words focused? What kinds of thoughts, emotions, and attitudes do your words create in you—and in other people? What kinds of responses do you receive from other people? Do they appreciate what you say?

REDIRECTED WORDS CHANGE YOUR EXPERIENCE

We've all heard the expression, "I want that word out of your vocabulary." Why? Because people understand the powerful impact of a word in the speaker's life and the lives of others. As you redirect your words—in your mind, in your speech—in order to pursue the type of godly speech for which Christians are to be known, you'll see that a kind word can go a long way in changing another person's experience as well as your own. As you redirect your words, you'll be redirecting your interpretation of your experiences.

If you want to change your life and see God work through you to change the lives of other people, you must begin to change your language. As you do so, you'll probably realize how many of your words are negative and corrupt and how those words—in speech and in thought—influence how you feel, think, behave, and handle failure.

I love to speak to groups, but invariably I experience a wave of nausea before I speak. I interpret this as part of the excitement that accompanies the work I do. Other people who experience this same nausea call it dread and terror and choose not to open their mouths publicly. What is the difference between our responses? It doesn't seem to be the experience but the interpretation of the experience. There is a big difference between "I can't wait to . . ." and "I can't stand to. . . ."

In the movie *The Sound of Music*, one of the catchy songs centered around Maria's fears. Julie Andrews sang about her "favorite things," and the song ended with this line: "Then I don't feel so bad." You may not be a public speaker, but you can experience many things that make you "feel so bad." Some of them may even make you feel the deep-gut nausea I just mentioned. When you experience that feeling, what do you do? Do your words reflect how badly you feel? Or do you attempt to redirect your words so that you don't feel so bad?

The Greek word *peirazo* can mean "trial," "temptation," or "test." This word derives its meaning based on how the person responds to a given situation. The same stimulus can be a temptation if you allow it to lead you into sin, or it can be a test that you pass with flying colors. In reality, most people label their situations in terms of the worst scenario, not the best. So they focus their thoughts on troubles and worries, thereby forgetting their blessings.

Words are the tools that can make or break your life. When used with wisdom, even a single word can have a radical impact—perhaps changing the course of history.

The Old Covenant, for example, was symbolized when Moses took the blood of young bulls, sprinkled half of it on the altar, and said, "This is the blood of the covenant that the Lord has made with you in accordance with all these words" (Exodus 24:8). The New Covenant burst into history when Jesus, during the Last Supper, changed the sentence Moses had used. "This is *my* blood of the covenant, which is poured out for many" (Mark 14:24, italics added). The small two-letter word *my* ushered in the New Covenant, and nothing has been the same since!

PAUSE FOR REFLECTION

1. Describe a time when you used words to make someone laugh or be encouraged.

_____

_____

How did you feel about that time later?

_____

_____

2. List several people whose words have had great influence on you. For each person, list at least one word and describe its impact.

_____

_____

_____

3. Which situations tend to particularly irritate you?

_____

_____

What can you do to redirect your words when those situations occur?

_____

_____

_____

4. What does it mean to you to be "an imitator of God"?

_____

_____

_____

_____

17

Commitment, Repentance, and Godly Imitation

As you take charge of your life, determine what your commitments toward God, other people, and yourself should be. Repent from sinful thoughts and actions that conflict with those commitments. Learn from a godly Christian who has taken control of his or her life and is willing to help you take charge of your life.

I hope and pray that you will continue to take charge of your life long after you finish reading this book. It won't be easy. Distractions will come. You'll be tempted to listen to "old songs." People will let you down. You'll feel as if you aren't progressing fast enough. You'll still be hit with negative thoughts. You'll feel discouraged at times. But you'll be taking charge! You'll be discovering new, godly ways to live.

Expect obstacles to appear in your path, and determine that you won't let them stop you. God will remain true to His character and will empower you to pursue His will for your life. He will help you attain the new goals He has given you. He will love and comfort you in all circumstances.

The following three guidelines have helped many people continue to take charge of their lives long after they've read my materials or participated in one of my seminars.

ARTICULATE YOUR COMMITMENTS—AND SEEK TO MEET THEM

Effective business leaders know the importance of clarifying their core commitments—excellence, integrity, service, and so on. But this awareness of core commitments is sadly lacking (and is desperately needed) in our homes, families, and nation. Many people have little idea what their core commitments really are and don't understand the significance of those commitments.

If you are a Christian, you are committed to Jesus Christ. But what does that commitment really mean? How does it influence your personal commitments to yourself and other people?

If you are married, you are committed to your spouse. But what does that really mean when the relationship becomes strained? Recently I counseled a married couple considering separation. The wife did not feel that her husband loved her, cared for her, or was committed to her. So I asked him to write out in concrete terms a statement of his commitment to her. He wrote out specific commitments that he could fulfill each day. Statement after statement flowed onto the page. His list was truly the stuff out of which marriages are reborn!

To what and whom are you committed? Are you willing to pursue godly commitments in a disciplined way? To strive to meet them consistently in God's power and wisdom? Such commitment not only strengthens businesses, marriages, and nations, but it will radically affect your life, too.

Your commitments are absolutely unique. No one else will be committed to the people, purposes, and priorities to which you are committed in the same way. No one else will be committed to bringing the love and mercy of Christ into your spheres of influence in the way you do.

PAUSE FOR REFLECTION

1. List six of your core commitments, one per line:

_____

_____

_____

_____

_____

_____

2. Next write out what you are doing in practical ways to live out each core commitment in a godly way. What did you discover?

_____

_____

_____

_____

_____

_____

3. What changes might you make in your core commitments?

_____

_____

_____

SEEK RESTORATION WHEN YOU DON'T MEET YOUR COMMITMENTS

Once you've evaluated the core commitments you are determined to meet in order to take charge of your life and be the kind of person you believe the Lord wants you to be, your path is only beginning to unfold. Next you need to strive to meet those commitments and create a structure for dealing with your sin when you don't meet them. Let's face it. You won't always hit the mark you're aiming at, but you can keep improving!

Let's say a man named Bill is a master at making commitments but is thoroughly unsuccessful in keeping them. He makes a commitment to speak kindly to his wife, and yet he responds harshly to her sometimes. Should Bill give up on his commitment, believing it's unrealistic? Absolutely not! He made an important, valid commitment, but he continues to sin. What he can do to make things right parallels what we can do when we don't measure up to our godly commitments and need to be reconciled with God and other people.

Admit the Sin

First, Bill can swallow his pride and admit to himself that he is continuing to sin. That's an important starting place.

Confess the Sin

The next step is always the same and is never easy. He can confess his sin to God and to his wife and ask their forgiveness. He has wronged them. He shouldn't justify his failure, rationalize it away, or deny it. And he shouldn't become angry with people who care enough about him to stop him from exhibiting this sinful behavior.

We need to ask for forgiveness whether or not we feel like doing it. When we do something sinful, we need to make things right. Fortunately, God understands our weaknesses and that we are sinful. "If we confess our sins," John wrote, "he is faithful and just and will forgive us our sins and purify us from all unrighteousness (1 John 1:9).

Repent of the Sin

As important as forgiveness is, it's not the last step. Bill needs to repent. Repentance involves a change of heart and mind. It is the act of turning away from the sin and heading in the opposite Christlike direction. It's a vital step on the road toward attaining holiness and spiritual power.

It's not enough for Bill to be sorrowful concerning his treatment of his wife. He also needs to turn from his sinful thoughts and actions and reverse his direction—pursuing what is right, good, and true.

Unfortunately, many people have the wrong concept of what repentance is. I remember when Harold (name changed) came to me.

A former politician, he had gone to a resort area and picked up a man for homosexual purposes. The man he picked up, however, was an undercover cop. The resulting publicity destroyed Harold's political career and was threatening to destroy his personal life, too.

"Do you recognize your homosexuality as a sin?" I asked him.

"Yes!" he exclaimed.

"Have you repented of this sin?"

"Absolutely," he stated. "There's no question that I have repented of it."

But as we talked longer, I understood that he was not going to stop his homosexual activities. "When I say that I've repented," he finally confessed, "I mean that I will never, ever get caught and busted for doing something like that again."

What Harold meant by "repentance" is that he would be more careful, not that he would change his thinking and behavior. Rather than truly repenting, he remained committed to sin. Rather than learning how to relate in a godly way to men and women and replacing his sinful patterns of thinking and behavior with righteousness, he wanted to continue sinful relationships without getting caught.

True repentance involves actively turning away from that which you should not be doing and choosing a radically different godly path. To actively turn away from sins and habitual patterns that have been destroying your life and probably harming other people is one of the most important actions you can take. It's the only way to truly "right a wrong." True repentance can be most clearly seen when there is a need for restitution. In these cases, it's not enough to say "I'm sorry" or even "forgive me." A repentant person is willing to make a payback to right the wrong committed. Restitution shows the intensity of commitment.

When you repent, you are no longer hiding or rationalizing. You have set the tone for taking charge of your life. You have told yourself and others close to you that you affirm with the Lord that "sin shall not be your master" (Romans 6:14). You are not saying that you will no longer sin. Rather, you are saying that you will no longer be dominated by sin. You've found the Light at the end of the tunnel and are persistently heading toward Christ. At every impasse, you refuse to lie down and give up. Instead, you keep learning to confess your sinful behavior to God.

Fortunately, you and I don't have to remain in our sins. Romans 6:14 reveals that sin is no longer our master. Our sins no longer have control over us. Our lives do not have to be dominated by sin. Why? The Holy Spirit gives us the power to resist the devil. God rules our lives and enables us to take charge over our sins.

Yes, we will sin sometimes. The Bible tells us that we are liars if we say that we have no sin in us. But through forgiveness and repentance, we will become more like Christ. We will "put off [our] old self" and "put on the new self, created to be like God in true righteousness and holiness" (Ephesians 4:22, 24).

As we seek to be godly, we'll have to deal with our old patterns of thinking and behavior. But when we continually choose to acknowledge our sin, ask for forgiveness, and repent, we are establishing new response patterns that will become easier to live out as time goes on.

Teaching yourself to "put on" new godly words and actions in order to break habitual sinful patterns of thought and action is a bit like breaking a new trail in the snow on our farm in central Ontario. The first pass is tough, but as I drive the car up to the house again and again, the snow packs down. Likewise, your habitual sinful patterns need to addressed again and again. As you continually address them, the path will become easier to travel.

PAUSE FOR REFLECTION

1. Think about your life right now. From whom do you need to ask forgiveness for sinful words and actions?

_____

_____

_____

_____

2. Determine the best way(s) to contact each of those people and ask for forgiveness. Be specific!

_____

_____

_____

3. Why is it important for you to confess your sins to God (1 John 1:9) and ask the Holy Spirit to help you repent of sinful words and actions?

_____

_____

_____

FIND A GODLY "TAKE-CHARGE" PERSON AS YOUR MENTOR

Perhaps you were reared in a family where certain sins were common, so you naturally perpetuate those same sins because you've never known anyone who did things differently or was willing to teach you biblical ways of responding. You may need a mentor who can help you learn better ways of responding.

Perhaps you already are using what you have learned in this book to take charge of your life. But you'd like to bounce ideas off a godly person who can guide you through difficulties you encounter and choices you must make.

Perhaps you are a new Christian who doesn't know the Bible very well. You need someone to help you discover how to study the Bible.

Perhaps you are battling depression and find it tough to maintain a clear perspective on almost everything in your life. You need someone to help you sort out important issues and encourage you to take the right steps that will help you move out of the depression.

Through the years I've come to realize the importance of having at least one wise, godly person standing beside me who believes in me, is seeking to know God better, is taking charge of his life, and who will hold me accountable to meet my core commitments. (Just because I teach doesn't mean that I am an island! In fact, I am reminded daily that I need to keep my feet firmly planted on the Rock—Jesus Christ.)

THE VALUE OF AN INSIGHTFUL COACH

The first time I decided to jog, I laced up a pair of tennis shoes, stepped out into the 95-degree heat and what felt like 200 percent humidity, and blasted off. Well, you can imagine what happened. I lasted about three hundred yards, developed symptoms of heatstroke, and fell exhausted into a bush containing poison ivy! My desire was strong, but I didn't know how to execute the exercise of jogging.

Running for exercise is not just about taking off down the street. It requires the right clothing and shoes, warm-up exercises, and exercises for cooling down. Today, two decades after my plunge into the poison ivy, I run every day of the week except Sunday. But it's amazing, as I look back on that rough start, that I have kept at it. That one bad experience could easily have been the *only* one. And it certainly took me much longer to learn the basics of running than it should have because I didn't take time to learn from other people.

Many people never jog again after an initial experience like mine. Similarly, many people who make take-charge commitments often lack proper planning and execution. It's not surprising, therefore, that they drop out of those commitments not long after reading motivational books or attending seminars.

So what might I have done differently when I started to jog? I should have thought, *If running is what I want to accomplish, and some people do this well, I need to find a good runner who is able to teach me what running is all about.* I should have learned the principles first before facing unnecessary failure.

Have you watched a winning athletic team practice? During each practice, excellent coaches train the team members, showing them exactly what they have to do and motivating them to excel in doing those things correctly. A player's every false move is scrutinized so that team members can correct mistakes, focus on right actions, and do those actions smoothly and properly—individually and as a team.

The apostle Paul, who faced many challenges in life, recognized the value of imitating the right people and pursuing the right moral influences. He challenged the church to imitate his behavior and that of the other apostles. He also challenged us to "be imitators of God" (Ephesians 5:1). He urged us to imitate what is good, lovely, and right (Philippians 4:8-9).

Was Paul being presumptuous when he wrote that the only way to obtain the peace of God that passes all understanding was to live a life exactly like his? No. A godly life is not an accident. A person is taught and trained in how to be godly. Sad to say, most godly people in the church did not learn godliness through the teaching of other Christians but through trial and error. This is wasteful, costly, and dangerous.

The secular world knows this. That's why every good sports team, for example, has at least one coach who teaches the athletes the finer points of the game—how to swing, how to pitch, how to block, how to break away, and so on. Likewise, the church needs coaches—models who can hone the skills of its members and help them successfully live the Christian life.

If you want to develop godly biblical habits that will become an integral part of your life, find Christians who can demonstrate clearly what these behaviors are—from their own lives and from Scripture. If you were to look right now for someone you could model yourself after in your quest for a godly life, there is no question about the type of person you'd seek. You wouldn't be too impressed with someone who had a million dollars but whose life was a mess. You'd look for someone whose life was filled with the fruit of the Spirit: love, joy, peace, patience, kindness, goodness, faithfulness, gentleness, and self-control (Galatians 5:22-23). These qualities make up the inner reality of the consecrated child of God and are available to you. In the same way, you'd be quite taken by someone who, regardless of his or her outward success (or lack of it), was able to handle life's struggles and difficulties with a God-given confidence and a hope.

Are these traits only inner mystical qualities that only spiritual elite people can attain? No. They are available to you and me. God has given you considerable control over your behavior. Whether or not your life possesses godly traits depends on whether you allow the Holy Spirit to produce His fruit in you. If you sit around and believe that it's someone else's responsibility to love you, for example, you'll always feel loveless. If you want a changed life, change it by taking charge of your life. Think and do things that are joy filled, love filled, and so on. Think of how you can please others rather than how others can please you. Make it your responsibility to love other people.

As we've seen, God has made it possible for us to be filled with joy at all times. Remember what Paul said? "I have learned to be content whatever the circumstances" (Philippians 4:11). He then added that the "secret" lies in trusting Christ, who gives us strength. You are capable of taking every situation in your life and representing it in a way that will facilitate joy or despair. The choice is in your hands. There's no reason to become mired in the muck. Remember, you have the power to focus on what is good, beautiful, true, and so on. Or you can focus on what is bleak and ugly. It's *your* choice!

If you want your inner life to lead to behaviors that accurately portray what it means to be a child of God, you can move in that direction—starting today! You can be a Spirit-filled person who doesn't need escape routes in order to find a meaningful life. And you can learn a great deal from someone who walks in godly ways and has learned quite a bit about how to be the man or woman God calls him or her to be.

The Bible is full of examples of people who pursued God and His path—and those who didn't. It tells us what happened as a result. We can learn from these examples.

Are you willing to study the Bible and learn from people who went before you? Are you willing to seek out a godly woman or man who can help you learn to apply God's Word to your life? Are you willing to seek out someone who has faced and overcome the challenge you are facing? And if you cannot locate such a person, are you still willing to seek God with everything you can muster and look to Him to guide you?

If so, do it!

PAUSE FOR REFLECTION

1. List three godly character traits you most admire and would desire to have in your life:

_____

_____

_____

_____

2. List at least one person (and preferably several) who truly exemplifies each of these traits:

_____

_____

_____

_____

3. Go to these people one at a time and speak to them about the trait(s) you'd like to develop. Ask them if they are willing to guide you in becoming more like Christ. Learn from them. Imitate them. As you apply what you learn from God, the Bible, and these godly people, your life will change!

4. Choose several godly men and/or women described in the Bible whose lives you'd like to study:

_____

_____

_____

_____

Now determine which one you'd like to study first and read about him or her. Carefully think about the person's choices, mistakes, joys, sorrows, and so on, and how these relate to your life and the lives of other people around you.

A FINAL WORD

As our time together draws to a close, remember how much God loves you and is willing to empower you. In His strength, you will do far more than you ever thought possible. You will climb the peaks in your life and enjoy and learn from the valleys, too. You will change the words you think and speak and the ways you respond to people and circumstances. God's hope, peace, and joy will fill you as you walk with Him each day.

Thank you for allowing me to enter your life in this special way and share truths that God has taught me.

> Rejoice in the Lord always. . . . The Lord is near. Do not be anxious about anything, but in everything, by prayer and petition, with thanksgiving, present your requests to God. And the peace of God, which transcends all understanding, will guard your hearts and your minds in Christ Jesus. (Philippians 4:4-7)

Notes

CHAPTER 1:
THE STARTING POINT

1. Seligman, Martin E. P., *Learned Optimism* (New York: Pocket Books, 1990), 55.

2. I'm not saying that people never need help from antidepressants or other drug therapies. But biochemical approaches—except in instances of clear biochemical, neurological, or organic etiology—perpetuate victim mentality, endorse an illness model for behavior, and do not require individuals to take personal responsibility for themselves.

CHAPTER 7:
FACING YOUR CHALLENGES

1. Matthew Henry, *A Commentary on the Whole Bible*, vol. 3 (Tarrytown, N.Y.: Fleming H. Revell, 1986), 394.

2. *Military History*, 3, no. 6 (June 1987), 10, 56-57.

CHAPTER 10:
WHEN THOUGHTS OR CIRCUMSTANCES
SEEM OVERWHELMING

1. *Book of Psalms for Singing* (Pittsburgh, Penn.: Crown & Covenant Publications, 1973).

CHAPTER 12:
UNLEASH THE BIBLE'S
TRANSFORMING POWER THROUGH SONG

1. *Book of Psalms for Singing* (Pittsburgh, Penn.: Crown & Covenant Publications, 1973), 119.

Index